The Story of
Father Marie-Joseph Lagrange

The Story of
Father Marie-Joseph Lagrange

Founder of Modern Catholic Bible Study

Bernard Montagnes, OP

Translated by Benedict Viviano, OP

Paulist Press
New York/Mahwah, N.J.

Edited for the American edition by Shirley L. Wagner

Cover design by Sharyn Banks
Book design by Lynn Else

Photograph of Father Lagrange used with kind permission of the École biblique, Jerusalem, Rev. Father Jean-Michel de Tarragon, Superior of the Priory of St. Stephen, Jerusalem

Originally published as *Le Père Lagrange* by Les Éditions du Cerf, France. English translation copyright © 2006 by Paulist Press, Inc.

Library of Congress Cataloging-in-Publication Data

Montagnes, Bernard.
    [Père Lagrange, 1855–1938. English]
    Father Marie-Joseph Lagrange : founder of modern Catholic Bible study / Bernard Montagnes ; translated by Benedict Viviano.
        p.   cm.
    Includes bibliographical references.
    ISBN 0-8091-4333-X (alk. paper)
    1. Lagrange, Marie-Joseph, 1855–1938. 2. Biblical scholars—Biography. 3. Modernism (Christian theology)—Catholic Church. 4. Dominicans—Biography. I. Title.

BX4705.L253M6613 2005
220'.092—dc22
                                                      2004028019

Published by Paulist Press
997 Macarthur Boulevard
Mahwah, New Jersey 07430

www.paulistpress.com

Printed and bound in the
United States of America

Contents

Contents

TRANSLATOR'S FOREWORD

The struggle within the Catholic Church for responsible academic freedom inspired by St. Thomas Aquinas is best exemplified in the twentieth century by the life story of the Dominican Father Lagrange. Because his story deals with the application of historical critical methods to the Bible, it is particularly sensitive, and the struggle of his peer, priest-scientist Pierre Teilhard de Chardin, is arguably less important in comparison to it.

Church autorities sometimes encourage scholars, sometimes penalize them. It condemned the scientific work of Galileo in the seventeenth century. It is not surprising that it blocked the publication of Father Lagrange's commentary on the Book of Genesis in the twentieth century. Another biblical scholar, Alfred Loisy, was excommunicated and his works were placed in the Index of Forbidden Books; he continued his studies in defiance and disobedience *outside* the Catholic Church. To avoid trouble during the church's campaign against Modernism, other scholars, such as Father Minocchi and Father Semeria, dropped their biblical studies altogether and turned their considerable talents to tasks in the fields of diplomacy and social work. Father Lagrange was the chief scholar who continued to pursue his biblical studies *within* the church. His work is responsible for keeping the flame of biblical studies alive in a time of darkness. After his death and his posthumous vindications (1943, 1948, 1965), the tiny flame he had kept alive would become a blaze, a bonfire, a conflagration. Father Lagrange was a frontiersman, a scholarly pioneer, who lit the beacon and opened the way to future studies in theology within the church.

Because of the importance of Father Lagrange's story, it has been told several times, notably by F. M. Braun and by Father Lagrange himself in his *Personal Reflections and Memoirs* (see the bibliography at the end of this book). What is new and different about the Lagrange biography written by Bernard Montagnes? Its specificity. Based on contemporary documentation, letters and diaries, Montagnes's version gets beneath the surface story to the personal feelings and thoughts of the principal characters at the time the events were occurring. Montagnes spent several years in original, archival research in France, Italy, and Jerusalem and wrote numerous books and articles on Father Lagrange. Listed at the back of this book, his scholarly works are richly documented and tailored for the academic reader. Having completed his scholarly work, Montagnes then wrote a short biography, without footnotes, for the general public. *The Story of Marie-Joseph Lagrange* is the English translation of Montagnes's short biography for the general reader.

Although the reader's patience may be tried at times by the many written exchanges between the major figures of the story at their moments of great crisis and anguish, acute focus is the price exacted by precise, careful historical scholarship. Effusive language detailing agonies of conscience and groveling declarations of obedience and orthodoxy may exasperate the reader further. The content of the story itself may make the reader uncomfortable. The period between 1903 and 1914 was a sad, painful one for Catholic intellectual life. But this is history as it happened, this is an historical disclosure of heroic sanctity. (The cause for the beatification of Father Lagrange has been introduced by the French Diocese of Toulon-Fréjus, with the support of many French bishops.)

Father Lagrange's commentary on Genesis—the introduction, the commentary on the first six chapters, the articles on the Patriarchs and on the Flood, which were denied publication throughout his lifetime—have all been preserved in page proofs. Father Montagnes reports that the complete manuscript of the commentary on Genesis survives in the archives of St. Étienne. Several factors strongly support the publication of these texts. Their publishing is merited as an act of reparation for the harm done to Father Lagrange and to Catholic intellectual life, for the historical record of critical analysis and interpretation of scripture (exegesis), and for the published record of Father Lagrange's role as exegete during his lifetime. The precedent for publication has been set. Analogies from Judaism come to mind. The commentaries of Benno Jacob and Umberto Cassuto, both on Genesis and Exodus, were published in English long after the authors' deaths. Although not current at the time of publication, they are of real help in analysis and interpretation. It has proven true that if Father Lagrange could write a book and get church permission to publish it, then others could write on the same subject and have their work passed by the censors. The experience of Father Lagrange's brilliant disciple, Joseph Bonsirven, provides an example. His remarkable thesis on rabbinical Judaism was turned down in 1912. In 1930, Father Lagrange published a book on the same subject. Bonsirven's work was published shortly after in 1935. To date, Father Lagrange's major work on Genesis has not seen the light of day. Does it follow that a Catholic published no major critical commentary on Genesis during the twentieth century? Logically, there is no causal connection, but psychologically there may be one.

The reader should realize that while this biography is thorough in regard to the major crises of Father Lagrange's life, it is far from exhaustive. For example, it does not tell of Lagrange's desire to write a book on the kingdom of God in 1907 to meet the challenge of Johannes Weiss's work. Such work was ruled out by the censors at the time, so Father Lagrange channeled his research into a book on messianic beliefs. Fifty years later,

Bonsirven fulfilled his teacher's wish by publishing the first modern Catholic exegetical work on this topic in 1957. Not all Father Lagrange's major publications are mentioned in this book.

Another sensitive matter is the role of Jesuits in the story. The reader should realize that during Father Lagrange's lifetime, many Jesuits supported him, even if they could not always do so openly. Others opposed him, especially Leopold Fonck. Today, the relations between the biblical scholars of these two orders are quite good, as are relations between their two graduate schools, in Rome and in Jerusalem.

In matters of translation, perfect consistency has not been sought in frequently recurring titles and names. St. Étienne is the same as St. Stephen. École biblique is the same as the Biblical School in Jerusalem. The head of the Dominican Order in Father Lagrange's day was known as the *master general*; today, he is referred as the *master of the order*. A larger Dominican house is usually referred to in English as a *priory*, occasionally as a *convent*, and loosely as a *monastery*. The Institut de France houses five academies; the best known is the French Academy, concerned with French language and literature. The Académie des inscriptions et belles-lettres is concerned with history. The École biblique refers to the archaeological school in Jerusalem. The other three academies concern the fine arts, natural sciences, and philosophy and political science. Finally, in French, the abbreviation *Mgr.* for *Monseigneur* is prefixed to the name of a bishop and also to the name of an honorary prelate. The latter is known in English as a *Monsignor* with the abbreviation *Msgr.* This difference has been retained in this translation.

Thanks go to those who undertook a preliminary translation: Sister Mary Joan Dyer, CPPS, Orsoline Chiappetta, Elizabeth Miller, Jennifer McCarthy, and Soteria Foufounis. Sister Mary Joan produced the final computerized form of the translation. May their generosity not be forgotten. The responsibility for any errors is mine alone.

Benedict T. Viviano, OP
Fribourg, Switzerland
September 21, 2000

PREFACE

This book speaks about a battle that lasted a lifetime and about the courage of a believer concerned about the honor of the church. Driven by a passion for truth and a great love of the Bible and of the church, Father Lagrange wanted to open the book of the scriptures to Catholics by releasing it from the sanctuary and exposing it to the open air, by causing it to be rediscovered as the rooted and living *Word*. He had to pay the price for it, that of suffering and renunciation until the end of his life, as this book testifies. But he did not suffer in vain, because for a century biblical research and published studies have multiplied, and now the Bible is more at the heart of the community and missionary life of the church and of the spiritual life of numerous believers.

Marked by Lacordaire's ideal of freedom, with a pioneer spirit at once daring and realistic, Father Lagrange ventured into a new frontier, that of the scholarly study of the biblical writings. He did it with great confidence in reason and in the Bible, with the profound humility of the scholar and of the believer. At the turn of a new century, faced with new questions, he wished to count on a critical and rigorous approach to biblical texts and to integrate the new tools of knowledge procured by modernity. He was convinced that this alliance was possible, that it could bring only honor to the church and profit to all, believers and nonbelievers. The new questions and their difficulties could not be avoided or put off until later: You had to have the courage to face them directly, in the very name of faith and the coherence of truth. The vitality of believing experience itself called for a renewed understanding of the foundational writings.

In committing himself to this way, Father Lagrange joined a long line of Dominicans who used all the resources of knowledge of their time so that the Bible would be better read, understood, contemplated, announced, and thus bear fruits of conversion. For an order, founded in the thirteenth century, which was called Friars Preachers, the Word of God must be at the heart of its apostolic and community life. From its beginnings, some friars set to work by giving greater importance to instruments of work that permitted greater access to the scriptures: concordances, translations, commentaries, textual criticism, studies of ancient languages, and so forth. One thinks about the group around Hugues de St.-Cher in Paris in the year 1230, but also about friars such as Simon de Hinton and Richard Fishacre teaching exegesis at Oxford itself, which particularly delights me! The necessity of knowing Oriental languages and of better understanding the culture and the milieu of the origin of the Bible led several to the Holy Land and to the Middle East where priories had been established. Some friars took the initiative of making the first translations into popular languages—French, Italian, English, German, Castilian—or they collaborated in it. I want to emphasize also the role of the biblical lector who, in each priory, was charged with reading and commenting on the scriptures for all the friars. The work of preaching and theology could not be realized without a serious biblical foundation, which required that one set to work to establish the texts and forge the tools that preachers, students, and professors need.

Father Lagrange took up this tradition and renewed it by making use of a study of the terrain, in the very land of the Bible, and by taking into account new knowledge acquired from historical, linguistic, archaeological studies, and so forth. He did it in an apostolic perspective, attentive to the spiritual framework of the study and careful to further a larger distribution and a greater love of the scriptures. The Biblical School of Jerusalem and the *Revue biblique* were born—and still pursue this effort—without counting all the works written by those who studied and taught there, and that greatest enterprise—*The Jerusalem Bible*.

When questions are new and complex, the service of truth needs time and freedom: It is necessary to explore trails without knowing the answers in advance. A man of science and of faith, wagering as did Thomas Aquinas on the mutual fecundity of critical thought and faith tradition, Father Lagrange had to confront the resistance that every new enterprise meets when it surprises, disconcerts, or simply unsettles habits. In the midst of the Modernist crisis, the atmosphere in the church was rather a fearful reserve or a marked hostility toward a project such as that of Father Lagrange. Opposition came from several sides: believers, scholars, religious groups, Roman congregations. They were borne by diverse motives, from fear to prudence, not to mention ignorance, incomprehension, opportunism, and multiple combinations of reason and of unreason. Several did not understand the stakes, or felt their faith threatened, or confused tradition and routine. His order sometimes vigorously supported him, but, it must also be recognized, sometimes upheld him only timidly. Father Lagrange, however, continued his way, in courtesy and serenity, as a true *gentleman*, avoiding provocation as well as servility.

Father Lagrange also received support from brothers as well as from diverse believers, priests, scholars, and members of the hierarchy who indeed saw the urgent necessity of his work and recognized in him someone solid in his faith and in his research. He himself was a team player and a community man. He had the fortune and the joy of being surrounded, supported, and loved; without that he would not have been able to go through all these harsh struggles, as he did, without bitterness or breakdown, while remaining until the end a man of prayer and of faith, attached to the church and to his order. It was in the very name of his ecclesial and religious commitment that he courageously bore a demand of truth and fidelity. All along his stormy route he continued to write and to study, in spite of the atmosphere of suspicion and blame of which he was the object. Today, he is proposed to be recognized by the church as "Blessed." He surely is so now, but at the beginning of the twentieth century, several would have been more than surprised!

A hundred years ago at Jerusalem, several religious modestly set out on an astonishing adventure with very few resources and little support, but with a true passion and a keen awareness of the needs of their time. They wanted to reopen the old Book to read it with great care, in its place of origin, and to have its message resound. Between the enthusiasm of research on the texts and the polemics they gave rise to, between the archaeological walks and excavations on the lookout for signs, between trips to Rome or elsewhere to sustain the Biblical School, Father Lagrange and his collaborators succeeded in opening new avenues in the church—because they held on in trust and were supported, because they knew how to listen at length to hard questions in the patience of intelligence and the fervor of hope.

I thank Friar Bernard Montagnes for giving us access to this passionate and often sorrowful journey of Father Lagrange. With great honesty in making us hear the witnesses themselves and the shock of their voices, he makes us enter into the heart of a debate that has not ended. The honor of the church and of the order still calls us to pursue our work in the fruitfulness of new knowledge and the faith tradition with exactitude and trust. The courage of Father Lagrange gives us the taste and this book permits us to grasp its difficult paths.

Father Timothy Radcliffe, OP
Master of the Order of Preachers
Rome, March 7, 1995

INTRODUCTION

Despite the high esteem in which Father Lagrange is held by biblical scholars, the man himself remains hidden. Being a humble servant, he was always careful to efface himself, giving primary importance to the school and to the scholarly journal that he had founded, or to his published writings. The early bibliography drawn up in 1943 by François Marie Braun includes 1,786 items published by Father Lagrange and is not exhaustive. It was only at a later date that Maurice Gilbert completed the massive bibliography. The *Revue biblique* that Lagrange founded in 1892 proclaimed from its beginning that it was "published by the Practical School of Biblical Studies established at the Dominican Convent of St. Étienne de Jérusalem." More recently, editorial credit was given officially to the *French* Biblical *and Archaeological* School, further submerging the recognition of Father Lagrange's work. Now that the cutting edge of biblical exegesis has been sharpened, it is time to bring the founder to the foreground. Neither his scholarly contributions nor his fierce struggle to have the historical-critical interpretation of the Bible accepted by the Catholic Church can be ignored. As the Modernist crisis shook the old Roman edifice, Father Lagrange held fast to his scholarly pursuits.

The same principle of publishing restraint applies to the life of Father Lagrange as to the life of Father Lacordaire: Certain chapters of their stories were so delicate that for a long while they were suppressed. Just as questions concerning proper observance had brought Father Lacordaire's followers into mortal conflict with each other, so decrees by the pontificate of Pope Pius X had led some members of the Company of Jesus to combat Father Lagrange with frenzied persistence. Brought to the knowledge of the public, these stories would risk reopening old wounds not properly healed. Censors and Dominican superiors seemed to have held these considerations in mind when in 1953 they refused to authorize the publishing of Louis Hugues Vincent's *Life of Father Lagrange*. Again in 1964, when Pierre Benoît considered publishing the *Souvenirs personnels* (Personal Recollections) of Father Lagrange, he had to ascertain that neither the authorities of the Dominican Order nor the authorities of the Biblical Institute would use their veto. Today, the historian, without obsessive fear of timeliness, can tell the story of Father Lagrange's struggle and service freely. The archives, save those of the Holy Office and, by a regrettable consequence, those of the Biblical Commission, are open. The essential source in researching the life of Father Lagrange remains the private correspondence, a portion of which was published in 1989 in *Exégèse et obéissance* (Exegesis and Obedience). It is upon this original source that I continue to rely for this portrait of the scholar and of the believer.

Bernard Montagnes, OP

Chapter I

FATHER LAGRANGE: THE FORMATIVE YEARS

Family Heritage

Father Joseph-Marie Lagrange, founder of the École biblique in Jerusalem, was born Albert Lagrange at Bourg-en-Bresse, France, on March 7, 1855. He was the fourth child of staunchly Catholic parents, Claude-Pierre Lagrange and the former Élisabeth Falsan. For two-and-a-half years, Albert's father had held the ministerial office of notary for the region, although the family roots were not in the department of Ain. These circumstances played a large role in shaping young Albert.

Rural Burgundy was the home of the Lagranges, while the Falsans resided in the burgeoning city of Lyons. At that time, unless there were exceptional circumstances, a farmer's son from Burgundy, such as Albert's father, even if he were prosperous, would not have been an acceptable suitor for the daughter of a highly regarded Lyons merchant family, such as the Falsans. The exceptional circumstance presented itself in the form of a dispute between Élisabeth and her parents.

Under the tutelage of the Jesuits, Élisabeth had developed a strong Christian fervor and aspired to a religious life. She preferred the Convent of the Sisters of St. Vincent de Paul, who were at the service of the poor, to the Convent of the Sisters of the Sacré-Coeur, who were at the service of her own middle class. On several occasions, she had served daily soup to the needy at the Convent of the Sisters of St. Vincent de Paul, and it was at their convent that she found the greatest sense of inner peace. Her family frowned on her service and on her choice of vocation. Neither the Falsans nor her mother's family, the Niepces, would support Élisabeth in her desire to break with the family in order to enter religious life. For Élisabeth, they chose marriage rather than the convent. Finally, weary of the struggle, Élisabeth gave in. She consented to marriage only on the condition that her suitor might be a believing and practicing Christian with whom she could feel united on a religious level.

Albert's father, Claude-Pierre Lagrange, had suited Élisabeth's requirements. He was a practicing Christian and had been a student of theology. The two met through Father Souaillard, a Dominican and a friend of Claude-Pierre's from his student years at the seminary of Autun. Father Souaillard had encountered Claude-Pierre in Lyons and enthusiastically agreed to plead his marriage suit before the Falsan family.

Élisabeth was dubious. Although sweet and passive by nature, she demonstrated a streak of stubbornness and would not be rushed into marriage. After thoughtful consideration, Claude-Pierre agreed with her wishes and promised not to bring up the subject of marriage again, if the Falsans did not support his suit. The Falsans were not pleased with the proposal of marriage, but the family patriarch, Dr. Potton, whose family were leaders in Lyons manufacturing, was not the least opposed. With Dr. Potton's blessing, the young man of thirty-six years and the young woman of twenty-three years married on May 1, 1850.

Between 1852 and 1870, Élisabeth gave birth to nine children. Only five survived—Louis (1852), Albert (1855), Pauline (1858), Thérèse (1862), and Marie (1870). Of the survivors, Albert's health was so poor that Élisabeth was alarmed at his fragility. Already having lost two children, she was tormented by bouts of poignant melancholy and overcome by a mood such as that expressed by a musical composition of Gustav Mahler, *Kindertotenlieder* (Laments of the Dead Children).

The sensitive Albert became aware of his mother's deep sense of loss in his late adolescence. As he approached his eighteenth birthday, Élisabeth took him into her confidence. Albert remembered the instance clearly. "One day, opening her writing desk before me, she showed me some faded white flowers, medals, toys in a box, remembrances of her children, all dead at an early age. 'Poor mothers,' she sighed, 'this is all that remains to them.'"

Albert's formative years were spent largely in the company of his mother and sisters, and a strong bond developed among them. The influences of his father and brother were not as strong. He was in their company less frequently. His father was occupied with his position as regional notary most of the day, and his brother Louis, three years older than Albert, pursued other interests. Albert often found himself in the company of his Potton cousins, all of them lively individuals, who would play major social roles in the life of the region. The oldest was Olympe (1852), followed by Charlotte (1853) and Albert (1854). Albert Potton would later become the French consul at Antioch, where he would receive his cousin and childhood friend Father Lagrange. Albert Lagrange's Falsan cousins were to achieve social status as well. His cousin Thérèse (1860) would marry François Ferier, who would purchase a deluxe edition of *L'Évangile de Jésus-Christ*. Amélie (1869) was to become the wife of Max Frachon. Amélie's wholehearted support for Father Lagrange led him to bequeath to her his rosary belt. Albert's youngest cousin, Pierre, was born in 1874. Among his sisters, brother, and cousins, Albert knew the joys of a numerous but united family.

The feminine predominance of Albert's family circle greatly marked his sensibility, stimulated his taste for drawing and music—he took up the cello—and prompted him to compete in needlework. His brother Louis was never far away and the two shared a brotherly affection. "We were always very attached to each other, never leaving each other during vacation. We had the same studies, the same entertainment, the same affection for our parents." As the two were going their separate paths, Louis to join the army in Algeria and Albert to take holy orders, they met at

Fort-National (Algeria). Albert wanted "to show him [Louis] my affection at the time that I, too, was going away from home."

Whatever the cause, Albert's relationship with his Lagrange relatives in Burgundy was not as intimate. "As a child, I saw no difference in the family relationships. Burgundy being farther away—it was necessary to go by carriage from Mâcon— we saw one another less—that's all."

Father Cormier, master general of the Order of Preachers, was impressed with Father Lagrange's Catholic background when the two met in 1907. "The cardinal of Rheims assured me several years ago that your family had provided you with a solid spirit of faith." Bishop Luçon, retired bishop of Belley (1888–1906), agreed. He was aware that Father Lagrange's parents had considered higher service. Married, they had created an exemplary Christian household.

The story of Albert's birth and baptism had been repeated to him fondly by his doting mother. Born in 1855 on March 7, [in those days] the feast of St. Thomas Aquinas, he was carried five days later, on March 12, to the baptismal font at the Church of Notre Dame. There he received the sacrament under the name of Albert Marie Henri—*Albert* after his Falsan godfather, *Marie* to show devotion to the Mother of God (and because of his god- mother), and *Henri* because of the family's attachment to the count of Chambord, the Bourbon legitimist heir to the throne. As customary, newly baptized, he was presented at the altar of the Black Madonna, where his life was consecrated to Mary. Because Élisabeth had already lost two children, she placed him under the special protection of the Virgin: "Mother placed me under vows for three years, dressing me in blue and white in honor of Mary. What a sweet thought! Do you suppose it is the source of Mary's special care for me?"

Christian tradition was Albert's family heritage, but he was also influenced by the Christian traditions of the Diocese of Belley. He was impressed by such figures of sanctity as Pierre Chanel, Julien Eymard, Sister Rosalie, and Jean-Marie Vianney.

In 1858, at the age of three, his family took him on a pilgrimage to the shrine at Ars, and in August 1879, he made the decisive retreat at the Charterhouse of Sélignac. All of these events led to his choice of a Dominican vocation.

Life within the diocese also permitted Albert to form lasting and trustful relationships with a number of prelates. These relationships helped to shape the course of his life journey. He became acquainted with natives of the area such as Bishop Sevin, bishop of Chalons-sur-Marne, then archbishop of Lyons, and with those who had received part of their formative training with the diocese, such as Monsignor Ireland, archbishop of St. Paul in the United States. He met those who would govern the church. Monsignor Richard (1872–1875) became the Archbishop of Paris. Bishop Soubiranne (1880-1887) would permit Father Lagrange to receive the Order of Subdiaconate in his diocese. Monsignor Luçon (1888 to 1910) would send a priest as a student to Father Lagrange's newly formed École biblique, but Monsignor Luçon's successor, Bishop Manier, judged this priest a "modernist" for having studied with the Dominicans of Jerusalem.

In 1858, when a wave of infant mortality was at its height, Élisabeth, fearing the worst for her son Albert, took him to the saintly Curé of Ars. This pilgrimage gave rise to two stories, one flattering, one sobering. Albert's sister Thérèse Lagrange told the embellished version reported by Father L. H. Vincent. She maintained that shortly before her mother's death, she had told her that the Curé of Ars had prophesied: "The child will not die. One day he will become a light of the church." Madame Lagrange would never have repeated these words to Albert. In keeping with her character, she would have sought to spare him the temptation of pride. The second story of the incident, told by Albert himself, was more sober. In a passage from his *Journal spirituel*, written during a convent retreat of September 1892, he says: "My parents took me on pilgrimage to Ars, where the holy pastor blessed me and perhaps cured me of a weakness of the intestines."

Father Vincent, who for forty years was the closest friend and most intimate confidant of Father Lagrange, shows an exemplary discretion in his summary. He writes: "If the future of the child and his role in the religious movement of this [twentieth] century were manifested to the prophetic eye of the saint and by him revealed to Madame Lagrange, none, other than her son, ever received the confidence, and they both carried the secret to the grave."

What remains indisputable is the fervent devotion to the shrine of Ars and its holy pastor that Father Lagrange held. During the summer of 1878, he made a pilgrimage to Ars with his mother. There he asked for the grace to die a Dominican, and a martyr. He returned there the following summer in the company of Pierre Batiffol to prepare his entry into the novitiate of St. Maximin. When, in 1891, he undertook the building of the École biblique in Jerusalem, he deposited a fragment of the cassock of the Curé of Ars in its foundation. Later in 1934 at St. Maximin, he offered a rosary that had belonged to the Curé as a gift to the mother of a young priest who lay dying. In 1935, to another Dominican colleague, he presented a relic of St. Jean-Marie Vianney, placing him under the protection of the Curé of Ars.

Education

The childhood of Albert Lagrange unfolded in a happy family environment. The family head, Claude-Pierre, although very affectionate, was intimidating and little inclined to confidences. As Albert recalled, "he was not very communicative." Claude-Pierre's reserve inspired tenderness as well as respect. "I knew that I had a very big place in his heart," Albert wrote. "He was the head of the family in the most traditional sense of 'Old France.'" Claude-Pierre was a resolute man with an energetic nature, able to defend and protect his family, made to govern and administer the household. His frankness imbued his sons with a sense of honor, to which Albert would attach a great value. Of clear-minded intelligence, Claude-Pierre dealt with business in a decisive way and without regret. A self-made man, he became a notary at Bourg, a legal counsel to the diocese, and a member of the parish maintenance board. "A Christian to the depths of his being," as Albert described his father, Claude-Pierre was strictly faithful to church observances. In politics, he was a liberal, a reader of *The Correspondent*, in the opposition at the time of the plebiscite in 1852. He was, however, more often busy with study than present with his family.

Albert's mother, *frail Élisabeth*, as they said of her at the time of her marriage, was a domestic woman, devoted to making her family happy. She ruled over them with tenderness. Formerly, she had had a passion for painting, but she renounced it to exercise her artistic talents by furnishing her home. Her gentleness was such that she perceived only the good and the beautiful. The negative and the ugly eluded her. She drew her strength from prayer, but her spirituality was shaped by her practical youthful experiences in Lyons. In rearing Albert, she lacked neither intuition nor firmness. From Albert's infancy, she had had a kind of vision of his priesthood, and early on, she had also noticed his attraction to the study of history. When Albert was a seminarian at Autun, she had coached him to show strength. When he was a Dominican novice, she had exhorted him to show humility and obedience. From her, the young Father Lagrange hardly risked inheriting the art of fund-raising or of making money yield a profit. "When I became prior in November 1907," he confessed, "the finances started going down immediately."

The warm family intimacy enjoyed by Albert lasted only a short while. Élisabeth would have preferred that Albert be educated in the elegant style offered by the Dominican School at Oullins, but at the start of the school year in 1864, Albert entered his seventh-grade class at the seminary of Autun. His father Claude-Pierre and his Uncle Louis, the parish priest, had studied there, and his older brother Louis had been studying there since the year before. Although Albert's father had not wanted to educate his sons to become parish priests, from early on, he had intended to turn their education over to these excellent educators who had been his fellow students at the very same desks. In his eyes, nothing was more valuable than a simple, strong, academic education, the kind he himself had received at Autun. Every day except Sunday, the students at Autun wore blue smocks. In winter, they wore clogs in place of shoes. The tough discipline at Autun was thought to form sturdy, independent personalities. Academic standards were high. (In his fourth year, Lagrange learned the Gospel of St. Luke by heart in Greek.) In-depth knowledge of Latin, Greek, German, English, and Italian was expected, and the sciences were not neglected. Geology, a nascent study at that time, had a place of honor at Autun. During the summer of 1872, Albert was particularly interested in the related field of archaeology.

As Albert remembered, "The teachers at the minor seminary in Autun brought us up, without boasting about it, in a tradition of simplicity and uprightness, and without exaggerating supervision, in an atmosphere of honor and honesty." Lagrange paid them homage in dedicating to them his *Critique textuelle* in 1935. He declared himself *olim parum docilis* (formerly not easy to handle); a severe or disapproving glance by an authority figure was capable of shaking him to his foundation. Yet Albert was not a dilettante nor nonchalant in his study. His shyness led him to take refuge in reading. He read Shakespeare rather than lounge about idly. He was fascinated by literature, and scholarly obligations did not prevail over his personal tastes. The result of his choices was not catastrophic. According to records from 1866 to 1870, he always received awards for honor and excellence as well as prizes in other areas.

Because the teachers at Autun wanted to develop a sense of personal responsibility in their charges, they practiced a system of free trust rather than severe discipline. "Had it been a system of suspicion, I would have done everything to escape," Albert reported. In giving the boys credit for good sense, the superior of the seminary was "not wrong in thinking that nothing acts more on the heart and the character, and that is what he wished to form.

Looking back on it all, his great trust made me avoid many faults: it would have been too unworthy to betray it," Albert declared. He adopted the system as his own.

Although some felt that literary foundations were emphasized above religious instruction at Autun, Albert regarded it as "a great grace to have been formed in piety at the minor seminary." A year after his entrance, he made his First Communion on the feast of the Trinity, May 27, 1866. Neither his ailing mother nor his father, who was at the side of his dying grandfather, was present. His godfather, Uncle Albert Falsan, was unable to attend. Young Albert received confirmation in the Fifth Class, on May 19, 1867. On the evening of his First Communion, he presented himself at the foot of the statue of the Virgin. "As after my baptism, Mary received me under her care. She has been the faithful Virgin." At this moment, he recalled, "I am certain I had heard the call of God....I was only thinking then of being a priest, without thinking of a special vocation." He was first attracted to the service of God during Second Class: "The day of the Annunciation [March 25, 1870] I had the revelation that I would enter the Order of St. Dominic." After taking the secondary school examination in March 1872, he returned to Autun, where he was in charge of the first communicants, to prepare for the competitive exam for entrance into the military academy at St. Cyr. The day of the feast, May 26, 1872, Albert had received a sign. "After communion, I walked beneath the cloister. Unmistakably, I heard a voice saying that one day I would take on the black and white habit of the preaching friars. I made a vow, without telling anyone, and I would remember it only later, when I had already carried it out."

Albert was the youngest of his companions. He did not feel pressed to make any life-forming decisions about his future. The notary studies at Bourg would fall to his older brother Louis, who afterwards preferred the military. Other perspectives opened before Albert. Perhaps he would become an engineer in the metallurgical industry, glory of Montceau-les-Mines, at a dozen kilometers from St.-Romain-sous-Gourdon? After a visit to Creusot, where his father had taken him during the summer of 1869 to see if he had a gift for machinery, Albert became apathetic and fell ill. Maybe he should become a lawyer instead and plead before the bar? Why not? The most appealing life seemed to him to be one devoted to public speaking, the most enviable glory, that of the political orators who guided the nation. Listening to trial speeches, which his father had him do at Dijon in July 1870, inclined Albert toward the law. Would he attend St. Cyr and devote himself afterward to the defense of his country? The Prussians had defeated France in the Franco-Prussian War of 1870, and Albert's generation nurtured a vengeance against them. Albert was fiercely patriotic, as were his countrymen. In his family, there were at least as many military caps as religious habits. His oldest brother, his sister Thérèse's husband, and his sister Pauline's son followed the military career path. At the St. Étienne of Jerusalem convent, while the consul of France was always met with appropriate protocol, the French military was met with the most enthusiastic welcome. Albert had taken the competitive exam for St. Cyr based on loyalty to the agreement he had made during secondary school examinations. It was for this reason he was eligible for entrance. "So great were my hopes for a career in public speaking, that the chances were very remote that I would accept admission." The study of law would require his moving to Paris, and mean a move upward in social status. While working at home in Bourg-en-Bresse, Albert registered for the first year (1872–1873) with the law faculty in Dijon.

By the end of Albert's teenage years, he had acquired most of the character traits that he would carry through life. His intellectual temperament and his aesthetic sensibility had made him a rigorous scholar. "At seventeen years of age, under the influence of my parents and of the minor seminary, my intellectual temperament and my approach to life had been formed." Albert's sympathies lay with the ideal of Christian liberty personified by Count

Montalembert, and he was repelled by the doctrinaire sectarianism of the newspaper editor Louis Veuillot. As for aesthetic sensibility, if the seminary had given him a taste for literature and rhetoric, his family environment had developed other perceptions, such as those he had inherited from the Falsans. His mother Élisabeth had loved painting with a passion. His Uncle Albert was also very artistic and had guided the tastes of his attentive godchild through learned commentaries on his stamp collections and on the art books in his library. During the last years that Albert spent with his family, drawing and cello lessons gave satisfaction to his artistic tastes. Finally, Uncle Albert had introduced him to geology, a science in which he himself was a master. From him, young Albert not only learned the scientific method of observation but also a rule of epistemology, the same rule that was adhered to by Claude Lévi-Strauss. What seemed to some to be in chaotic disarray, to the geologist had an underlying order, a master meaning, obscure, but understandable through transposition of its elements. Uncle Albert's lesson was one that the young Albert would remember and apply in the future.

Albert's Parisian years were rich in worldly experience, intellectual preparation, and religious fervor. Thanks to his experiences, Albert would not be one of those clergy that the satiric Lucien Febvre depicted. He would not be one of those who came out of high school to enter the seminary, who came out of seminary to enter the clergy, and who were ignorant of worldly resources and levers of power, as well as ignorant of a person's deeper instincts and powerful appetites. During his Paris years, Albert often attended Française and Pasdeloup concerts, went to art exhibits and museums, visited monuments and churches, or listened to parliamentary or religious masters of eloquence. He often strolled beneath the shade trees in the Luxembourg gardens while reconstructing the world in his head, as students often do. He was seen now and then at the racetrack at Longchamps and at Chantilly. He made light of his losses. "I very regularly lost at the pari-mutuel, and if I didn't lose a lot, it is because I didn't have a lot to lose." He was not, for all his adventures, a reveler. He resided at the Catholic Circle of the Luxembourg, directed by Eugène Beluze. He made his first attempts to speak in public at the Ozanam Conference, presided over by the Marist, Dulong de Ronay. He visited the poor assisted by members of the St. Vincent de Paul Society. He taught the catechism to the young Savoyard chimney sweeps.

At law school, where he obtained his law license before putting in a year of military service, he scarcely attended classes. He put all his effort into preparing for exams. Practical law did not interest him at all, but Roman law intrigued him because of its historical nature. Albert would have preferred an arts degree, which would have suited his tastes better than law, but which did not exist at the time. He registered at the Sorbonne, but did not present himself for a degree. He took Greek courses at the École practique des hautes études and appreciated their technical approach. Beginning in January 1876, he registered at the Institut catholique, where the law school had just opened. The exams for the Institut took place before a mixed jury, presided over by a state university professor, but held in a church university building. Albert received a doctorate of law at the July 1878 session. At last, he was free to follow his personal choice.

In the spring of 1877, a little more than a year before he received the doctorate of law degree, Albert had experienced a conversion that he had related in his unpublished *Journal spirituel.* "One day," he wrote, "when I was at the races at Longchamps, a friend told me there was a telegram at home. I went home immediately. The telegram brought bad news from my family. [His father was seriously ill.] Distressed, I entered the Church of St. Sulpice, and went to the back to Our Lady's Chapel. At the feet of Mary, I prayed a long time with fervor. [The *Personal Reflections and Memoirs* adds, "In leaving, I was never the same."] Several days later I bought a rosary, then I returned to Bourg."

If it had been left only to him, Albert would have entered the seminary at the beginning of the 1877 school year, but his father wisely judged that a doctor of law could render more service to the church in the then-foreseeable Modernist crisis. A year more in law school would confirm the wisdom of his father's advice.

Vocation

On several occasions from his attendance at the seminary of Autun onward, Albert had thought about becoming a son of St. Dominic. How did this calling reveal itself? Albert had been influence by the image of Father Dominic himself, as depicted by Fra Angelico and as presented by Father Lacordaire. "Ever since I had read the *Conférences de Notre Dame* and the *Vie de Saint Dominique*, the Dominican ideal dominated my thought. I gave myself to St. Dominic after reading the work of Father Lacordaire and after being completely captivated by the radiant image of the saint as seen in the *Coronation of the Virgin* by Blessed Angelico of Fiesole. I did not doubt the exactitude of this portrait, and it was indeed just what one might imagine, a loving vision of a pure soul. Long before entering his order, I was his son. I prayed to him every day." It was during the summer of 1878 that Albert made a pilgrimage to Ars to confide his Dominican vocation to the saint there.

Since Albert did not want to run the risk of failure with the Dominicans, he prepared for the novitiate by enrolling in a year of seminary training at Issy just outside Paris, from 1878 to 1879. He enrolled in an introductory course in Thomistic philosophy, taught by the Sulpician Pierre Vallet. "What our teacher knew best of Aristotle was the formula, 'A beginner must believe,' and he did not allow any discussion, while at the same time displaying great kindness to all." The same strictness that disgusted Batiffol forever after with Scholasticism incited Albert to study the text of St. Thomas attentively. At the school of the priests of St. Sulpice, Albert was initiated into a "sober piety, rather restrained than flaunted, touching the depths of the soul while avoiding sentiment." Such conduct was characteristic of the Sulpicians, in brief, a behavior opposed to emotional effusions. Like Batiffol, Albert would bear the mark of this spirituality for the rest of his life. Those years marked his first direct contact with the Bible. The year before, on the advice of the Sulpician Hogan, Albert had started to read St. Paul's letters in chronological order. At Issy he learned from the Sulpicians—teachers whose memory he would always venerate and to whom he would dedicate his commentary on Matthew in 1922—that he acquired "a passionate taste for the *Word of God.*" The year at Issy marked Albert's meeting with two other young men, both of them as aware as he of the pending crisis that was shaking Christian thought as it was being confronted by modern culture. All throbbed with apostolic ardor to serve the church on the most pressing battlefronts. "To you, Pierre Batiffol, the study of Christian origins! To you, Henry Hyvernat, the knowledge of the Christian Near East! To you, Albert Lagrange, biblical studies! We will be part of the school of the future, of the new school, of the school that will defend, by study and by scholarship, the holy ark of the church," asserted Batiffol in 1881. Was this just the boasting of overwrought seminarians? Not really. In 1889, Hyvernat would obtain the chair of biblical archaeology and oriental languages at the Catholic University in Washington. In 1890, Lagrange would found the École biblique—the Bible School of Jerusalem. In 1892, the *Revue biblique* would begin to appear in Paris. In 1898, Batiffol, already a successful historian, would become rector of the Institut catholique of Toulouse.

During the summer of 1879, a retreat at the Carthusian monastery of Selignac, as well as a pilgrimage to the tomb of the Curé of Ars, assured Albert Lagrange of his Dominican vocation. As Albert remembered it, "It seemed as though I walked in full light, as if God were showing me the way in the form of an ardent flame." It remained only to decide where he would enter the Order of Preachers. Neither Father Souaillard, who had brought about the marriage of his parents and to whom he had confided his aspirations, nor his Uncle Potton, to whom he was related by his mother's sister, were able to attract him either to Paris or to Lyons. "By my birth, I belong to the Province of Lyons, but certain rather hard words for Montalembert and even for Lacordaire had made a bad impression on my old liberalism, even in my feelings of a penitent Catholic." Albert was led to discover the beautiful Convent of St. Maximin, where the novitiate of the Toulouse province was located, and he went there to receive the habit of the Order of Preachers from the hands of the provincial, Hyacinthe Marie Cormier, October 6, 1879, under the name of Brother Marie-Joseph. A year later, on October 7, 1880, he vowed to obey St. Dominic and his successors, until death. Almost immediately afterward, on October 30, the brothers, expelled *manu militari* from St. Maximin, had to take refuge in Spain.

The Dominican formation transformed Albert Lagrange to such an extent that even his writing was changed. Many difficulties and many joys marked his inner transformation to Brother Marie-Joseph. He was distressed due to his exile so far from France at the Convent of San Esteban in Salamanca, where the Dominican students of St. Maximin were welcomed but where they were cut off from everyone and lacked everything. He had suffered the ordeal of the brutal transition from novitiate to rigorous study, from intense spiritual dedication to intellectual aridity. He had mourned the death of his father, Claude-Pierre, whom he had been able to visit during the summer of 1883, but who had died September 23, after Brother Marie-Joseph had returned to Salamanca and shortly before he was ordained Father Lagrange. At the time of his return, Brother Marie-Joseph was comforted by the Dominican life, as fervently observant at Salamanca as it had been at St. Maximin. He was soothed by the proximity of St. Teresa of Avila, venerated at Alba de Tormes, where the brothers went on pilgrimage several times. Brother Marie-Joseph remained ever after a faithful devotee of the *Madre*. Spiritual experiences, too, discreetly reported in the passages of his *Journal spirituel* that he reread, and annotated forty years later, calmed him. One early journal notation had been added during the course of his novitiate, on the feast of the Annunciation in 1880: "A sensible feeling of the presence of God in the soul, a true revelation added to faith." Another annotation was made during his retreat in September 1882, when, in experiencing the presence of Jesus Christ, he understood how grace connected him to the Savior. "It seems to me that I had never heard anything like it....I lived for several days in this light." He shed gentle tears on the evening of his ordination on December 22, 1883: "I say my first Mass Sunday the 23rd at the altar of the Holy Rosary, with the ineffable joy of serving communion to my mother and to my sister Thérèse."

Because of his year of studies at the seminary in Issy, Brother Marie-Joseph was placed in the Dominican theology department for the duration of the school year, 1880–1881. His first year in exile was lived at the subsistence level. Conditions of poor food and impoverishment were not favorable to intellectual life. During the following school year, the provincial Cormier entrusted major responsibilities to two young professors in their 30s, both of great personal worth. Étienne Gallais was appointed conventual prior, regent of studies, and professor of sacred scripture. Gil Vilanova was placed in charge of the teaching of dogma. His public conferences on theology aroused the enthusiasm of the people of Salamanca. "I understood him well, I, who was unable in dogma class to hold back my tears at the first hearing of his lucid, stirring words, whose entire eloquence was in the concise analysis of the articles of the Angel of the Schools [St. Thomas Aquinas]." Under the direction of these two men, Brother Marie-Joseph was guided in method and doctrine. According to their appraisal, the brother had acquired "admirable mental gymnastic technique, which makes him supple enough, and subtle enough to avoid lazy approximations and confused generalizations, and which no amount of erudition can replace. [These were indispensable traits for what was to come.] Critical thought must be neat and clear or else it is nothing but an accumulation of observations without relevance." With a passion that would not be quenched, Brother Marie-Joseph plunged into St. Thomas's *Summa theologiae*, at the very moment when, under the impetus given by Pope Leo XIII in 1879, Thomism meant "intellectual liberation." It meant leaving behind the ruts in which baroque Scholasticism was stuck and returning to the medieval tradition, to patristic and biblical inspiration. It had not yet become an imposed orthodoxy in twenty-four theses comparable to the decrees of the Biblical Commission. In short, it meant to consider St. Thomas as the harmonious conclusion of all Catholic teaching and not as the starting point for petty quarrels. "O, very pure Mary," Brother Marie-Joseph prayed, "teach me to combat heresies, not Catholics."

In 1881, the superiors had already decided that Brother Marie-Joseph was going to teach sacred scripture. A Hebrew Bible having finally arrived from France, Brother Gallais and Brother Marie-Joseph copied passages from it in order to learn how to read and write Hebrew. The Hebrew class at the university, which Brother Marie-Joseph received permission to attend, seemed more like a magic show than like philology. "The professor wrote the consonants on the chalkboard with flawless penmanship, then as if by magic, made the vowel points appear by means of certain mechanical recipes of which contemporary grammarians have lost the secret. 'Da gusto,' [It's a pleasure] cried one of my classmates. There was never a question about doing a translation." At this rate, Brother Marie-Joseph did not risk preparing himself to become a professor of sacred scripture. During the years 1884 to 1886 at Salamanca, after his ordination, Father Lagrange was in charge of teaching church history. At Toulouse the next two years, when the Dominican students had returned from exile, he was assigned to teach both philosophy and the Bible, without specialization. On the advice of Henry Hyvernat, with whom he continued to correspond, and Paulin Martin, he began to learn Syriac and Arabic on his own. At Toulouse afterwards, Father Thomas, professor at the Institut catholique, encouraged his solitary labor, introduced him to critical questions, and lent him indispensable works.

After these half-measures, the provincial council decided, in September 1888, to send Father Lagrange to Paris to study Near

Eastern languages. He would work with Father Vincent Scheil, an expert in Assyriology. But since the Dominicans of Paris were unable to house Father Lagrange, the provincial Colchen obtained from the master of the order permission to register him at the University of Vienna. He spent three semesters there, not for biblical exegesis (which he deemed a less profitable course for the moment), but for the acquisition of the philological basics and for an introduction to the methods current in the Germanic world. He took classes in hieroglyphic and hieratic Egyptian from Professor Reinich and classes in Arabic and Assyrian from Professor David Heinrich Müller. Professor Müller also introduced him to rabbinical exegesis and to the Mishnah. He benefited also from an Arabic course given at the School of Commerce. To his university acquaintances, he added a friendship with the prior of the Vienna Dominicans, Father Andreas Frühwirth, whose support would be valuable when the latter became master of the order (1891–1904), just after the founding of the École biblique.

To learn the languages of the ancient Near East when one is thirty-three years old, and finally to specialize after having completed so many studies, requires one to absorb a large amount of knowledge in a relatively short time. "I threw myself with ardor into these purely technical studies with all the more application because it was too late." Whoever does not begin languages early, Father Lagrange would repeat unceasingly, "cannot really master them. He can only have a smattering." Father Lagrange had to be content with that, to teach sacred scripture to young Dominicans at Toulouse, since such seemed to be his future. Then, on February 5, 1889, Lagrange received a letter from his provincial in Toulouse, which upset all his expectations.

Father Colchen had released Father Lagrange to the Priory of St. Étienne of Jerusalem to help found a school of sacred scripture there. A terse line written two days later in Father Lagrange's *Journal spirituel* gives us a glimpse of the confusion he felt. "My Jesus, it is a consolation to me to think that you have suffered this sorrow: *hic ure, hic seca, hic non parcas* [burn, cut, spare me nothing here]. Only spare me during eternity. It is indeed very hard to count on oneself for nothing and to count on you for everything!" More than thirty-five years later, when Father Lagrange was writing his *Personal Reflections and Memoirs*, he recalled this moment of distress: "I was shattered. Father Colchen's letter seemed to me to toll the death bell for my hopes. What could one do so far from the scholarly world? Would we be able to get the books we needed there? Would it be possible to work in that burning climate?" Not able to bear the uncertainty, Father Lagrange confided to his friend Andreas Frühwirth. Frühwirth was not very encouraging. "He shared my fears of the climate and of the difficulties of a foundation, of which I had finally spoken to him, and not without dread and repugnance."

Chapter II

THE FOUNDING OF THE ÉCOLE BIBLIQUE

The St. Étienne house in Jerusalem, where Father Lagrange was summoned to build a school, had been founded as a result of a pilgrimage of penance. This pilgrimage to the Holy Places had been organized by the Assumptionists and took place from April 28 to June 8, 1882. Father Matthieu Lecomte, a renowned Dominican preacher, had been invited to make this pilgrimage, which became known as the "pilgrimage of the thousands" due to the large number of participants it attracted. Originally from Lyons Province, Father Lecomte was much in demand as a preacher throughout France. He had appeared in the most prestigious pulpits and had often been invited by the bishops to preach at retreats for the clergy. He had entered the Order of Preachers in 1852, just after the only French Dominican Province had been reestablished (1850) under the direction of Father Lacordaire, its first provincial from 1850 to 1854.

When a division occurred among the disciples of Father Lacordaire, a division led by Father Antonin Danzas (provincial from 1854 to 1858), Father Lecomte was resolutely aligned with Father Danzas against Father Lacordaire. He had taken sides with a group of seven priests and two lay brothers who had met at Christmastime in 1856 to found a priory in Lyons; they called it a "reformed priory," or priory "of strict observance." This priory would form the nucleus of the future Province of Lyons that would hold the same strict aspirations. By their alliance, they felt they had chosen a lifestyle that conformed to the historical tradition of the

Dominican constitutions, taken literally. Father Lacordaire, they judged, followed the constitutions or ignored them as he pleased, taking into account times, places, and people and being guided by a desire for progressive adaptation. This division was not based exclusively on the manner of interpreting the text of the Dominican constitutions but probably centered on the fierce opposition to the political and democratic liberalism of Father Lacordaire. Proof of this liberalism is the invitation Father Lagrange received when he presented himself to the Priory of Carpentras in Lyons province: "Join us. You will see we are not liberals. We are leaving Father Lacordaire, Montalembert, and the others. We are following Louis Veuillot." Veuillot was a Catholic newspaper editor who advocated a Bourbon legitimist restoration of the monarchy in France. Father Lagrange understood that this thinking was not an isolated instance, but really a commonly held conviction. Not wishing to "follow Veuillot," he quickly turned on his heels and looked elsewhere.

When in 1859 Father Lacordaire, reelected provincial of France, and Father Danzas, then prior of the priory in Lyons, found themselves in competition to establish a house in Marseilles, Father Lecomte further aggravated their conflict by the impetuous zeal he displayed. For the rest, there was nothing to do but follow the instructions of the master of the order, Father Vincent Jandel, who asked that the fathers of Lyons cut the ground from under the feet of Father Lacordaire. The friars obeyed the orders of their prior, sending him to found a priory in Marseilles in line with the strict observance of Lyons. The results did not meet their expectations. The foundation of the priory at Marseilles had been delayed until 1862. Father Lecomte, who was preaching in a parish town at the time, was not invited to its inauguration. Encouraged by Master of the Order Jandel, tension reigned among the friars of the Lyons priory and the friars of the French province who were faithful to Father Lacordaire.

Now, in 1880, Father Lecomte, a fifty-year-old fighter, worn out by incessant work and affected by an inner weariness, attempted to lessen his activities. Limiting his preaching meant spending more time at his priory in Poitiers in the Province of Lyons. He then perceived that lack of sleep due to getting up at night for the midnight office, added to his lack of food from perpetual abstinence and frequent fasting, permitted little intellectual activity. The rigid monastic schedule broke up the day and contributed to his lack of study time. Under such harsh inconvenience, Father Lecomte underwent a critical change of mind regarding the regular observance on which the Lyons Province prided itself. The other friars never forgave him for this change. Father Lecomte began looking for an opportunity to escape both from his personal problems and from the internal dissension among the friars. To have sought transfer to another French province would have provoked the Province of Lyons, and the Lacordairean spirit of the Province of Paris did not attract Father Lecomte at all. To look for a position farther away would have suited his aspirations better, but that way had been cut off. The French parish in St. Petersburg had been assigned to another, and the French enclave in New York, which he had dreamed of evangelizing, had also been ruled out for him by the archbishop of that city, as well as by the Dominican provincial of the United States. Still the project of establishing himself elsewhere anchored his thinking. During a brief visit to the Basilica of the Sacré Coeur at Montmartre on November 25, 1881, he dedicated to the Sacred Heart of Jesus his future work, although he had not the slightest idea what it would be. Then in Jerusalem, in May 1882, Father Matthieu Lecomte received striking news: The Dominicans, formerly present in the Latin Crusader Kingdom in the Holy Land, planned to re-establish themselves in the Land of the Bible, preferably in Jerusalem. Their purpose would be to welcome French pilgrims who sought a French oasis in the Holy Land, particularly priests who wished to make a retreat there.

Almost as soon as it was born, the idea was realized. The moment the master of the order gave permission, Father Lecomte bought the presumed site of the stoning of St. Stephen and obtained from Pope Leo XIII the authorization to found a priory in that place where weary French pilgrims would find hospitality. Father Lecomte's future excavations there would uncover the remains of the basilica dedicated to the first martyr by Empress Eudoxia. For four years after he purchased the site, Father Lecomte made trips between France, where he gathered resources and recruited companions, and Jerusalem, where he began excavation, transformed an old slaughterhouse on the property into a priory, and envisaged the construction of a new monastery. His sudden death, on June 19, 1887, occurred in Jerusalem, plunging the Dominican community of St. Étienne into dark confusion. The friars were faced with a hard decision. Should they continue the newly begun work or abandon it? The vicar of the Dominican house, Father Paul Meunier, in the Province of Lyons, suggested a bold alternative: The order should establish a faculty on the site to teach Near Eastern languages and sacred scripture.

In Jerusalem, the idea of studying the Bible in the Holy Land was already in the air. The French government, when it had transferred the Church of St. Anne to the White Friars in 1878, had foreseen the construction of just such a graduate school. It had been envisaged as a place where six to twelve French ecclesiastics could gather to improve their knowledge of sacred scripture. Cardinal Lavigerie foresaw, with good reason, that the French bishops would recoil at the cost of the school and would send no one to enroll. He, therefore, did not pursue the school project. For his part, Father François Picard, superior general of the Assumptionists, dreamed, in 1887, of establishing at Notre Dame de France a school of sacred scripture where his religious would become competent and resolute adversaries of a menacing danger: "criticism, often so risky, sometimes even contrary to the Christian spirit." The Dominicans often affirmed that Pope Leo XIII suggested to Father Lecomte that he take advantage of the Jerusalem site to study sacred scripture, but that affirmation proves an illusion. Among the Dominicans, the project of using the grounds of St. Étienne for a house of biblical studies did not reach back further than 1888. At the time of Father Lecomte's death, they found themselves completely unequipped to undertake its realization.

In 1889, the master of the order was providing for the creation of a theological faculty at Fribourg; he could not be responsible for another institution in Jerusalem at the same time. There was nothing for the superior of St. Étienne to do but appeal to the three French provinces for help. The priories in Paris and Lyons answered tardily, but with kind words, that they had no one to send. Only Father Reginald Colchen of the Toulouse province responded quickly and positively: "In the Toulouse province, Father Colchen had the reputation of a saint, but not a professor. But, by the spirit of faith and because such was the vocation of the order, he favored studies with all his might. Perhaps also, being an Israelite by origin, he had a particular affection for Holy Zion." Guided by the general interest of the order, the provincial Colchen wrote to Jerusalem and to Vienna on the same day, February 2, 1889. He assured Father Meunier of his eager cooperation. He announced to Father Lagrange that he was placing him at the disposal of the superior of St. Étienne.

"Father Lagrange, whom I grant you," Provincial Colchen wrote to Father Meunier, "has applied himself these last four years to the study of Near Eastern languages in their application to the teaching of sacred scripture, which is his specialty. To this end, he is at present engaged in Vienna, in special studies under the eminent professors Reinisch and Müller. At the end of the academic year, he could very well move to Jerusalem and, after a year devoted to the study of Palestine and its monuments, he would be, I believe, apt to offer one of the courses for the new faculty."

When Father Lagrange overcame his initial shock, he laid out a teaching program that would require four years and several professors to complete. In his plan, liturgical celebration, with the exception of the midnight office, would supply the spiritual framework in which biblical study took place. Tersely, he noted support for the project in his journal: "One, for the spirit of the order and the blessings of God; two, for the nourishment of supernatural faith, for we ought not create dangerous apostates; and three, for its effect on the religious populations of the Near East." Father Lagrange would share his intellectual and spiritual program with Father Meunier a few days later. To the superior of St. Étienne, he insisted that the friars assigned to Bible study should be steeped in liturgical prayer: "I believe I have given proof of a true passion for study, but I declare that I do not understand it as possible, in our order, without assigning a large part of the office, to rest and light!...The study of holy scripture without a great spirit of faith is very dangerous, as proven by numerous apostasies, and I do not want to work in order to arrive at that sort of result for myself and for others."

Father Lagrange's last doubts were erased after his third semester in Vienna, when the master of the order, at the request of the provincial Colchen, authorized his visit to the Holy Land. Provincial Colchen wrote to Rome on January 18, 1890: "Father Joseph Lagrange, at the beginning of February, will finish, in Vienna, the study of ancient Near Eastern languages, which he has gone there to study. I ask your permission to let him complete these studies by a trip to the Near East that will include Egypt, Palestine, and Lebanon." Father Lagrange was granted six months, until the end of August. He embarked at Trieste (February 14), stopped off at Alexandria on Ash Wednesday (February 19), and visited Cairo for fifteen days. He arrived at Jaffa the third Sunday of Lent (March 9), "in very bad weather." There he was welcomed by a lay brother from Jerusalem, "who," he notes, "had come to find me at the boat, fearing that I would not have the courage to get off." By the next day, Father Lagrange had arrived in Jerusalem, where he stayed more than four months. He did not leave again until mid-July and returned to St. Maximin at the beginning of August.

Father Lagrange left few words about his first contact with the Holy Land. For the first time, he celebrated the end of Lent and the Easter cycle of the resurrection, the ascension, and

Pentecost in the holy places where the mystery of the salvation took place. Of these experiences, not one confidence or record survives. After Easter, Father Lagrange rejoined the French pilgrims in Nazareth. Guided by the Assumptionists, he visited Galilee and went up with them to Jerusalem. Among the pilgrims were two Dominicans from Toulouse and one from Paris. According to one published account, on May 18, the Sunday after the ascension, Father Lagrange delivered an eloquent discourse during Mass before the French consul on the ruins of the Basilica of St. Étienne. Before leaving Palestine for Lebanon, he was even able to take part in an archaeological exploration beyond the Jordan. He was accompanied by a priest of the Latin Patriarchate, Abbé Heidet, who was smitten with archaeology, and a Jesuit specialist in exegesis, Father van Kasteren. The trip was not without scientific merit. At Madaba, Father Lagrange had made an imprint (a *squeeze*) of a Nabatean inscription that later became the subject of his first scholarly publication in the field of Oriental languages.

From the outset, Father Lagrange was overwhelmed by his experiences in the biblical lands, dazzled by the beauty of the country and moved by its traces of history: "I was stirred, seized, gripped by this sacred land, given over to delights of historical sensations of far-off times. I had so loved the Book and now I contemplate the Land!" This time he had felt convinced: "Not a doubt existed in my mind on the rightness of doing biblical studies in Palestine." He wrote to the master of the order: "The future practical school of higher biblical studies could not find a more appropriate place than Jerusalem, the Holy City of the Old Testament, a city whose very crime makes it dear to all Christians, since they can follow there the scenes of the life and the passion of God." Even the chance circumstances of French politics were to work in favor of the project. The Lyons province envisaged sending their young novices to Jerusalem in order to withdraw them from three years of military service. (Novices were legally exempt from military service if they were assigned to the Orient for ten years.) Lagrange was also impatient with the delays by the master of the order and resented the wearisome uncertainty owing to the lack of a precise plan. He left Jerusalem for Lebanon on July 15 in the company of Father Ollivier, without knowing when, or if, the hoped-for school would be realized.

At the beginning of August, however, the master of the order, after weighing the respective recommendations of Toulouse, Fribourg, and Jerusalem, decided to send Father Lagrange to St. Étienne. He did so based on the favorable comments of Provincial Gallais of Toulouse, who had counted on Father Lagrange to teach dogma. The faculty at Fribourg had reported with enthusiasm that they had already announced a course by Father Lagrange on St. Matthew, and the authorities of Jerusalem pled that without the presence of Father Lagrange there would never be a biblical school. Father Lagrange responded with restraint. "I was completely abandoned to obedience, but precisely for that reason, I did not want to take the initiative in a difficult work when I was not sure I could turn the matter to the honor of the order. I asked for a formal precept." The answer came in the form of a license, given at Rome on September 29, appointing Father Lagrange chief lector in charge of studies in the House of Studies at St. Étienne of Jerusalem. By the same license, Father Séjourné was appointed professor of Holy Writ, and the status of Dominican *studium* was granted the school by the same act. The day before, in an effort to respond to a request presented by the ambassador of the French Republic in the name of the minister of foreign affairs, the master of the order undertook to make St. Étienne a French priory and thereby place it under the protection of France. The priory would be subsidized like all other French institutions in the Near East and accredited to deal with Turkish authorities.

"We," wrote Friar Joseph Marie Larroca, master general of the Order of Friars Preachers, "declare and signify by these presents that the house of Friars Preachers, recently established in Jerusalem under the name of St. Étienne, is of French foundation and that, conforming to our intention and will expressed many times, it is and will remain exclusively entrusted to religious of French nationality, so long as France will be able to supply us to that effect with sufficient numbers of religious."

In the meantime, Father Lagrange left Marseilles on September 27 and returned to Jerusalem, where Father Séjourné had preceded him on October 6. The license sent by the master of the order arrived on October 15, and the three student friars sent by the Lyons province were now present, so the school could open in November. The course began on Tuesday, November 4, the day after All Souls, celebrated that year on November 3. The official inauguration would take place November 15.

For the opening of the Practical School of Biblical Studies, Father Lagrange gave a speech which one cannot call "suitable for the occasion" without devaluing it. Present were the school chairman and French consul general, surrounded by superiors of religious communities (White Friars, Trappists, Assumptionists, Fathers of Sion, and Christian Brothers), along with several representatives of the Latin Patriarchate and the vicar of the Melkite patriarch. Father Lagrange had inserted a rhetorical flourish at the end of his speech: "Strengthened by your sympathies, we will begin, with the help of Madame Ste. Marie and Monseigneur St. Étienne, in the confidence that God wills it!"

The speech presented the lofty goals of the École: "We must see to it that the Orient gets equal time with Greece and Rome," to restore, within the Christian culture, her place in Jerusalem, in short, to return to the Great Eastern Book which is the Bible. In order to understand the text of the Bible, we must draw on the land of the Bible. "One cannot understand the Bible without placing oneself in its atmosphere, without consulting both Hebrew and other Semitic languages, and without seeing the monuments, elsewhere than in museums, and the customs, other than in travel narratives." God, in giving us the Bible, has not invited human intelligence to babble on but to progress: "He has opened up to it an endless field of progress in truth." In a single paragraph, the word *progress* is repeated four times. "What I admire the most about Catholic doctrine is that it is at the same time immutable and progressive. It is not a restriction for the mind, it is a rule. It imposes itself on the mind, but it asks for the mind's participation. Great minds can freely give themselves over to their dominant passion and can still progress in the light. Revealed truth is not transformed. It grows. It is a progress because new acquisitions are made without taking away anything from treasures of the past. Thus, the history of exegesis is the most beautiful of literary histories." The Bible offers itself to a new investigation thanks to the resources of modern culture. "We who love all that our times love of the beautiful and the good, let us try to share with them their path. But the Bible could also become a battleground. On this battleground, we must not use a crossbow against a cannon; that is, we are invited to rival our adversaries in competence; to recognize in the Bible the word of man, written as history, and at the same time, to receive the Bible as the *Word of God*, bearer of transcendence. The two aspects are inseparable. In knowing it better as a history book, one enjoys it more as an inspired and divine book....Whether we like it or not, our century, by its almost excessive attachment to historical studies, will end up admitting the transcendence of the divine fact." The synthesis of rational research and believing, adherence to which the new school aspires, will be shown even in the arrangement of its future buildings, as the speech of Father Séjourné explains. When the Basilica of Eudoxia is rebuilt, "the new sanctuary will unite the priory to the school and will serve as their center."

In November 1890, there was nothing in the hall of the old slaughterhouse to encourage Father Lagrange's triumphant words. Still embedded in its walls were the rings where animals awaiting slaughter had been tethered. "It was in no way necessary that this project be Dominican," Lagrange went on, " and I admit, without false modesty, that it could have been entrusted to worthier hands....This is a common work for all the Catholic communities of Jerusalem. All of them have contributed to it....Messieurs, all of you have encouraged this work which we have humbly, weakly, above all, poorly begun, with only a table, blackboard, and a map for school equipment."

At the beginning, the École biblique found itself in a precarious situation. It lacked personnel, books, resources, and even statutes. The elementary means were missing. There were only four professors. Father Lagrange dealt with the Old Testament, Hebrew, and Assyriology. Father Séjourné, formerly a professor of Greek at the minor seminary of Sées in Normandy, who had volunteered for St. Étienne when Father Lecomte was present, would teach the New Testament. Father Doumeth, a Melkite priest who had entered the order for the St. Étienne priory, would give the course on Arabic, his native tongue. The Abbé Heidet, of the patriarchate, a Dominican tertiary, would teach introductory courses in history, as well as the geography of Palestine, and the topography of Jerusalem. He would also direct archaeological trips, since he had lived in Palestine for nine years. The Assumptionist Germer-Durand, of Notre Dame de France, and Father Cré, of St. Anne, would collaborate on public conferences on history and archaeology.

Father Lagrange suffered a number of disappointments at the outset. It became impossible to count on Abbé Heidet, whose share of work fell to Father Séjourné. Father Doumeth turned out to be such a poor pedagogue that he discouraged his students, and Father Lagrange had to take over part of his coursework. From a practical point of view, since Father Séjourné had only a competence in Greek and a familiarity with the country, almost everything depended on Father Lagrange. The situation improved temporarily when the Dominican mission in Mosul sent Father Jacques Rhétoré to teach Oriental languages from 1894 to 1898, before the disciples of Father Lagrange took over his work.

During its first year, the École biblique had only five students. Four were young friars from the Lyons province who would begin the cycle of Dominican studies. The fifth was a young Assumptionist sent from Notre Dame de France for the same basic training. In the early days of the École, Dominicans and

Assumptionists sent to Jerusalem to begin their formative studies constituted the main body of students. Father Lagrange puzzled over the proper course work. "It is a bleak horizon," he wrote of the student body in May 1891. "Only four young men, too young to follow biblical questions. The Assumptionists have begun to lose their eagerness. If we do not get some help, it will be a fiasco." Ten days after inauguration, Father Lagrange already knew where his main problem was going to be: "Our work has barely begun and is having a rough start, but patience. If we had enough students and money, all would be well. What I would like above all would be students from the order, already half-formed for theology, who could give themselves to languages and form a reserve for the future." Little by little, students who were already priests would come prepared for specialized studies, but never too numerous and never destined for the school. It was among the youngest that Father Lagrange would discover and mold his future collaborators: Antonin Jaussen arrived in Jerusalem on the first of July 1890; Hugues Vincent, August 11, 1891; Raphael Savignac, March 20, 1893; Félix Abel, November 26, 1897; Paul Dhorme, November 29, 1899; and Bertrand Carrière, March 20, 1902.

Because there was a shortage of staff members, each member was forced to hold a number of offices. Father Lagrange was already an overworked professor: "I teach four classes—languages—in the late afternoon and three—biblical science—in the morning, and I do not know if I can keep it up." His duties expanded when he became the superior of the house, first as vicar in April 1891 and then as prior in April 1892, with the primary task of builder. He accepted these additional burdens obediently, but not without complaint. The day after he accepted the vicar post, he commented to the vicar of the order: "I am persuaded that the responsibilities that you have placed on me will paralyze me almost completely for studies. Up until now people believed me to be as unsuited for administration as I was born to teach. I believe that they were right." He entreated Father Xavier Faucher, friend of Father Lecomte, to come to the aid of St.

Étienne, "afflicted since yesterday with a vicar who has no connection except with Babylonians and Israelites (the ancient ones, not the Rothschilds) and no experience except with grammar, so we are very much counting on you to fill the gaps." Ten months later, the weight of his burden overwhelmed him. "It is not without much reflection and without going as far as I could, that I have decided to entreat you to relieve me of my functions as superior of the Priory of St. Étienne....The reputation of St. Étienne has much improved, both in public and in the order, but its material situation is in a sorry state. Under these conditions, I do not have the freedom of mind that research calls for, nor the inner peace necessary to a superior." A little later, Father Lagrange made the same complaint to Father Faucher, to whom he expressed himself more freely: "Dear Father, pray for us that someone will replace me as superior. My time is eaten up. I can no longer study, and it is, above all, by study that I can be useful to St. Étienne." His complaint was a wasted effort. The master of the order had no one else to send and was planning to make Father Lagrange the first prior of St. Étienne once it was canonically erected as a priory.

Palestine in the 1890s was a poor country with a population of 650,000, of which only 15 percent were Christian—almost all were Greek Orthodox Arabs. The population of Jerusalem had doubled from 1850 to 1890 and numbered 40,000 inhabitants. About 80 percent were Jews or Muslims. The Christian population consisted of 4,000 Orthodox, 2,000 Latin, and a few representatives of other Christian groups, Catholic or not. The country offered no intellectual resources, such as libraries, and no resources of an economic kind. The collections made in Christian countries for the Holy Land were reserved for the Franciscans, so St. Étienne survived only on alms for its daily subsistence, or on loans meant for the construction of buildings. During a retreat in August 1893, Father Lagrange confided to his *Journal spirituel*. "I give you thanks for having placed me in true outer poverty, so that I must expect my bread, and that of others, only from your charity, since I cannot even count on my own labor." Even when the Priory of

St. Étienne had elected to have a prior come from Paris, a person whose contacts in Parisian society permitted him to rebuild the Basilica of Eudoxia, Father Lagrange remained reduced to begging. "You would do me a great kindness," he wrote to the master of the order in March 1898, "by sending me some money for books. I do not dare any longer to ask Father Prior, who is so absorbed by his constructions. I am deprived of the most necessary books. Here, there are no public libraries." During the first years of the École, had it not been for the alms procured in Paris by Father Xavier Faucher, the fathers of St. Étienne would not even have been able to pay the baker. Such were the sorry conditions in which Father Lagrange undertook his scholarly work.

The absence of any clearly defined canonical status intensified the mortgage on the future of the École. Because the personal work of Father Lecomte was pursued by other fathers and oriented to another task, the work of St. Étienne gave the impression, even inside the Dominican Order, of a private foundation, for which none of the French provincials was responsible. For want of a better solution, the work of St. Étienne was placed under the direct jurisdiction of the master of the order, but in fact, the whole weight fell on the local superior. Alone, Father Lagrange must see to the recruitment of staff, as well as to the financial administration. Even when St. Étienne had become a priory and was elevated to the rank of *studium*, things would not change in Jerusalem. Recognition would come but only after the First World War, a wait of fifty years. The master general of the order assumed the leadership of the St. Étienne project and the school was recognized by the French Republic as the French School of Archaeology in Jerusalem. From the point of view of church authorities, official recognition would have to wait almost one hundred years. In order to confer a doctorate degree, the École founded by Father Lagrange had to wait for the decree of June 29, 1983.

The miserable conditions that surrounded Father Lagrange did not prevent him from determining, with admirable lucidity, the main direction of the École biblique. His predecessors had planned to devote the house of St. Étienne of Jerusalem to the studies of orientalism and biblical studies, offering advanced teaching by a learned faculty similar to a university. In place of that, Father Lagrange founded a practical school of biblical studies. He took this path compelled in part by necessity. His inspiration was drawn from the epistemological model of the École pratique des hautes études in Paris, created in 1868. The school offered a fourth section in historical and philological studies, as well as a fifth section, in 1886, of religious studies. In a completely unexpected way, the intellectual model created by Duruy influenced the decisions of Father Lagrange. Remembering the Greek lessons given by Monsieur Tournier (the schoolmaster of Msgr. Duchesne), as well as visits to the manuscripts in the national library directed by Canon Graux, Father Lagrange noted in his personal memoirs in 1920, "This is what inspired me to found a practical school of biblical studies." Rather than teaching in rhetorical style, Father Lagrange wanted to teach through an experimental apprenticeship. One of the most brilliant students of the École after the First World War, Monsignor Bruno de Solages, recalled: "In historical-positive studies, it is the facts that must have the last word. That was Father Lagrange's precept: 'Look carefully at the text yourself. You should not say, "Father Lagrange has said it," because you will have seen it for yourself!'" To another student who busied himself taking notes instead of looking at the text under discussion: "But look at it! Don't take my word for it! It is with reason that when I founded the École, I called it the Practical School of Biblical Studies!" On one hand, the curriculum called for tireless study and analysis of texts through textual criticism and literary criticism of the writings and historical criticism of the narratives. On the other hand, the curriculum required the student to consider the relationship of the environment—geography, archaeology, epigraphy, and ethnology—to the text. Such was the program announced from the first day by the inclusion of the word *pratique* in the name of the biblical school.

At the end of two years, Father Lagrange confirmed the success of this practical approach to the master of the order. He wrote on July 8, 1892:

> I believe our resources are sufficient for the true goal of the work, which I have had a great deal of trouble maintaining against exaggerations. Some have presented our work as a complete university of Oriental languages. They are would-be friends. We have a *Practical School of Biblical Studies*. To use our time most gainfully, it suffices that we can make known the Holy Land and the Bible, with languages strictly needed for exegesis. Now, we have worked for two years, and if there are more complete universities in Europe, which is quite obvious, our work occupies no less a place apart: Nothing can take its place, and it can be very useful. This is what the scholars whom I have met understand wonderfully well.

It was necessary for the school to offer appropriate quarters. The two superiors who preceded Father Lagrange as head of St. Étienne understood this. Father Lagrange added another perspective: The school needed a conference room open to the public of Jerusalem (Christian or Jew) interested in the Bible. The construction of the building allotted to the school must precede the construction of Eudoxia's basilica, and it must precede the building of the present priory as well. It was Father Lagrange, appointed vicar of St. Étienne on March 23, 1891, who bore the burden of this enterprise, from the decision to the realization. In April 1891, he noted that the plans were "prepared on site by a skillful architect, M. Boutaud of Poitiers, who with me had taken all the measurements in three days, so that the school, the basilica, and the priory would be in harmony." On April 8, Father Lagrange foresaw an increase in cost to about 50,000 francs, not counting the 3,000 or 4,000 francs for absolutely necessary gratuities. On June 7, the contractor estimated a cost of 66,844 francs. According to 1891 accounts, the completed building would come to 94,368.29 francs.

Since St. Étienne did not have a cent available for this construction, Lagrange could not face the expense except through loans, adding the overwhelming worry of paying the interest and reimbursing the capital. "Father Lecomte," remembered Father Lagrange, "had dedicated the [school's] founding to the Sacred Heart." From the laying of the first stone appropriately on the feast of the Sacred Heart, June 5, to the occupation by the first friars on the eve of the Immaculate Conception, December 7, the work was completed in six months. December 8 became the feast day of the school.

Upholding the spiritual tradition in which he had rooted the school, Father Lagrange, on laying the first stone, had buried in the foundation, with the obligatory commemorative inscription, a series of medals and relics. He had listed the medals in his memoirs: the Sacred Heart, Our Lady of Lourdes, Our Lady of the Rosary, St. Benedict, St. Mary Magdalene and Pope Leo XIII. The house council minutes book contained a list of relics of the Lord: fragments of rock from Bethlehem, from Golgotha, and from the Holy Sepulchre, as well as a listing of relics of illustrious Dominicans. Among these relics was a fragment of the chasuble of Father Jerome Savonarola, probably a souvenir brought back from Fiesole where Father Séjourné had made his novitiate and his profession. Relics of Father Jandel, Father Lacordaire, and Father Besson, chief players in the reestablishment of the order in France, were also included. Father Jandel had created the new administration. Father Lacordaire had lent the impetus for restoration and directly inspired the Dominican vocation of Father Lagrange. Father Besson had died a saintly death in the Holy Land. The unexpected presence of a fragment of the soutane of the Curé of Ars among the relics attests to the personal devotion Father Lagrange held toward him to whom he owed so much. The heroic courage of Father Savonarola, the apostolic lucidity of Father Lacordaire, the priestly faithfulness of Father Jean-Marie Vianney, these are the hidden sources from which the École drew its spirit.

From 1890 forward, the École biblique and the Priory of St. Étienne were bound together in a common project. The Practical School of Biblical Studies is "established in the Dominican Priory of St. Étienne of Jerusalem." To take this phrase lightly would be to misunderstand radically the original design of Father Lagrange. The school finds in the priory its spiritual framework; the priory finds in the school its apostolic work. The two ideals remain just as inseparable in the person of Father Lagrange, at home both in the oratory and in the laboratory. "I love to hear the gospel chanted by the deacon at the ambo, amidst clouds of incense: Then, the words penetrate my soul more deeply than when I find them in a discussion in a learned journal." Without confusing academic and religious goals, the prayer of the scholar and the quest of the believer complement each other and meld into a single life experience.

Chapter III

THE WIDENING INFLUENCE OF THE ÉCOLE BIBLIQUE

To lock himself up behind the walls of St. Stephen, with two or three amateur professors and a few beginning students, did not fit Father Lagrange's bold plan. He was aware that Catholics were not going to be able to evade the "biblical question," as it was labeled, following a famous article by Mgr. d'Hulst in January 1893. The scientific interpretation practiced by the Protestant universities across the Rhine would collide head-on with the teaching traditionally dispensed by the Roman Catholic Church in the matter of the Bible; he knew and understood that the meeting would bring about a painful crisis in Catholic thought. He was convinced that the dogmatic tradition of the church, on the condition that one not exaggerate the affirmations, was compatible with an exegesis not strictly literal, one broader and more progressive than the current study. Orthodoxy, contrary to what Renan claimed, did not oblige one in any way to believe that the biblical books were the works of those to whom their titles attribute them.

Secularized biblical criticism and the teachings of the church—were they compatible? To show a positive proof of this compatibility, Father Lagrange would have to confront both traditionalists, who saw him as an enemy within the gates, responsible for introducing the wolf into the sheepfold, and progressives, who saw him as an acrobat, refusing to submit to the demands of criticism. To face the crisis, he had to hold together the two ends of the chain: accepting the Bible as the Word of God and playing the role of "thoughtful critic."

"Accept the Bible as the Word of God": Nothing expresses the theological inspiration of Father Lagrange's approach better. He sets out his program in the first issue of the *Revue biblique* in January 1892. Biblical exegesis is rooted at the outset in faith, is practiced for the benefit of faith, and reaches its conclusion in a viewpoint of faith. Different from the explanation by Loisy, the interpretation practiced by Father Lagrange does not stem from pure scientific curiosity, free of all religious influence. Within his theological perspective, theological faith makes use of historical criticism, just as Thomas Aquinas uses Aristotelian philosophy as an instrument of understanding. Father Lagrange does not put faith in parentheses; he does not practice a secularized reading of the Bible; but a *believing* reading. He adheres to this belief even though it is commonly held that such criticism has the function of sacrilege. His attitude has its source in a preunderstanding that he has not stated explicitly, but with which his thinking is impregnated: The true result of biblical revelation will not contradict the truth discovered by the historical critic. Father Lagrange regretted not being in a position to advance greatly this fundamental reflection on the coherent status of truth, learned from Thomas Aquinas. "I truly wish that the good Lord had given me more genius to do the work that is necessary to be done in order to reconcile public opinion with moderate criticism, but I do not feel that I have either the strength or the aptitude for that. Detailed exegesis is one thing, broad views [are] another thing." His preference, however, led him to difficult questions. What does the inspiration of the biblical writings mean? Why can a Catholic recognize several documents in the Pentateuch? How ought he to profit from the historical method?

To play the game of criticism thoroughly would be to renounce the false securities of the Catholic community. Here would flourish an archaic science, a Catholic exegesis for internal use only, one with an epistemological status comparable to the Marxist biology of "the grasses of unhappy memory" (Lyssenko). "What one would then pass off as Catholic exegesis," wrote

Father Lagrange in 1904, "would do as much harm to our faith as rash innovations and would tend to create a state of mind that would not be worthy of the intellectual honor of the church." Catholic exegesis ought, by the power of its competence, introduce itself into the international scientific community, make itself recognized in the world of "foreign" (non-Christian) scholars, like Maspéro or Clermont-Ganneau, those "savants of the Institute," whose esteem meant so much to Father Lagrange. Someday he would deal with these men as equals. That was his goal "in the interest of the church." All scientific inadequacy would be exploited against the church. After having attended the Congress of Orientalists in Geneva in August 1894, "I was very well received," he noted, "but I saw again all that we need to do to equal those scholars."

When Father Lagrange wrote that "the nonsense of M. Fillion does as much harm to the church as the audacity of M. Loisy," and when he did not hesitate to accuse a publication of "dishonor to Catholic scholarship," although it had been approved by the Master of the Sacred Palace, he showed that a scholar does not have the right, through party spirit, to praise to the skies the mediocre productions, more pious than true, of those who believe they are serving the church. Lagrange saw himself accused of aligning his sympathies with those of the independent scholars, of reserving his severity for his own coreligionists. He explained, with regard to the independents, "I must recognize the extent and the value of their work. Historical-critical scholarship is elaborated and practiced in the universities: that is the fact against which we cannot revolt, but from which we have to profit. To be sure, the publications of the universities need to be discussed, but following the rules of justice and of courtesy. Certain persons, accustomed to rough polemics, do not realize that politeness does not lessen the value of fundamental objections. Far from it." Thus, in regard to Catholics, Father Lagrange preferred silence to polemics. Thus, in regard to Pierre Batiffol, faithful friend, devoted collaborator, and prolific contributor to the *Revue biblique* (thirty-nine articles published), he preferred to pass over disputable work. "Reservations," he explained, "when they are formulated, remain below the truth, even if they hurt authors too accustomed to the incense that *Semaines catholiques* lavishes upon them. Biting irony, even in moderate doses, only works against tough and unfair adversaries."

Father Lagrange fought for the honor of "good studies" in the church, as he liked to say. What could be more heartbreaking, he thought, than the doctrinal lack of culture, the intellectual incompetence, the scholarly inadequacy of the clergy? "I am too passionately attached to the Roman Church not to hope that we emerge from the situation of intellectual inferiority where we now are on certain points. The obvious value of the new methods, which imposes itself on my mind, and an ardent desire to contribute to our getting out of our dishonorable stagnation are also contributing factors."

To make the position of the school better known became, from then on, an urgent imperative, which Father Lagrange planned to tackle through conferences of popularization, through specialized publications, and through participation in scholarly meetings.

The "biblical and archaeological conferences of St. Stephen," organized from 1891 to 1892 on, "offered the advantage of having competent Palestinologists from Jerusalem collaborate with the professors of the École." The first year the Abbé Heidet of the Latin Patriarchate, Father Cré of St. Anne, and Father Germer-Durand of Notre Dame de France collaborated with Father Séjourné and Father Lagrange, to give seventeen public conferences between December 7, 1891, and April 11, 1892. These meetings enabled the École to win hearings with audiences broader than its regular student body. Those in attendance were not only educated Catholics, such as consuls, doctors from various hospitals, the Communities of St. Anne, the Fathers of Sion, the Assumptionists, and more rarely the Franciscans, but also the Greek Orthodox and even the Jews, among whom they had some success. "They even wrote an article in the Hebrew newspaper in which they invited their coreligionists to come," a young Assumptionist recounted in January 1891.

With Father Lagrange's growing public image came a growing number of invitations, some modest, some flattering. In 1900, at the seminary of Belley, Father Lagrange reported to the master of the order on May 12: "The superior has asked me to give a biblical conference to his students, which I have done before more than one hundred very sympathetic seminarians and professors. I will look for similar occasions in other seminaries with the idea of making prejudices fall, and to find some students. It is absolutely necessary that this year the current flow toward St. Stephen." Rome responded in a rather reticent manner. "If I could have responded immediately to your letter of May 12, I would have recommended that you use a great deal of discretion in accepting biblical conferences, and to use extreme prudence in the terms of your lectures. The hearers are not all benevolent and some interpret badly the most inoffensive words." Outside of Jerusalem and the Holy Land, Father Lagrange would have willingly satisfied the invitations that were addressed to him from Paris, Brussels, and even the United States of America. His Roman superiors, however, showed themselves resolutely hostile to this form of outreach.

The idea of founding a highly specialized journal struck Father Lagrange. Scarcely four months after the inauguration of the school, he submitted the new project to the master of the order. On the need to create a specialized journal of biblical studies, he explained that all the specialists in the field agreed:

These questions are so vital for the church, and have so developed, the heterodox have done so much on this ground, that the necessity imposes itself on Catholics to treat these questions at the rate of the attacks and of the discoveries, and yet in a deeper manner. The readers of the general reviews cannot sustain this serious tone. Recently, the editor of *La science catholique* and of *Le prêtre* asked me to write some of their articles half-joking, half-serious, omitting the foreign names that frighten the French reader! I hastened to refuse, preferring fifty serious and specialized readers to readers who want mainly to be entertained. It is up to us to take the initiative and to provide the editorship: The enterprise is nothing but honorable for the order. One could ask if we are up to the task. There again, since the founding of our school, we have an exceptional advantage...The work of a review, although very hard, is less difficult, less daring than the foundation of the school, because we will find ten collaborators through writing before finding one who would come to collaborate on site.

As Father Lagrange conceived it, the review must respond to three conditions. The first was rigor: "What we must absolutely win is to be taken seriously by competent men." The second was pluralism: "It ought to be open to collaborators outside the Dominican Order so as not to become the monolithic expression of a single corporation." The third was theological: "It will always include an article of theological even mystical exegesis, because scripture is, above all, the *Word of God.*"

In Paris, Xavier Faucher found a publisher (Lethielleux) the for the projected publication and became its editorial secretary for the first three years. The *Revue biblique* was launched without delay. The first issue, dated January 1892, arrived in Jerusalem on December 30, 1891. The volume of 1892 offered the writings of five Dominicans, three Jesuits, two Italian Barnabites, one White Father, an Assumptionist, a Sulpician, and ten secular priests. It had suffered from the hasty circumstances of its birth. "It lacked homogeneity, resembled a *Festschrift,* and its contributions did not come from qualified specialists. It is not profound enough," observed the great Austrian Dominican scholar Heinrich Denifle. These flaws, attributed to youthful exuberance, where quickly remedied by the new secretary, the precise Batiffol, a new publisher, Lecoffre, and the scientific exactness of Father Lagrange. Rome showed mistrust: "Our poor *Revue*," moaned Father Lagrange, in May 1893, "is caught between the carelessness of the publisher and the suspicions of Rome, which have been intimated to me in very harsh terms." Father Lagrange did not intend to deviate from the foreseen orientation. The instructions he sent to the secretary were unambiguous. They could not allow themselves to be muzzled on burning questions, but should keep a rein on eager young collaborators (such as the Italian Barnabite Semeria, whom Father Lagrange estimated as "excellent," but who was still at the stage of green fruit). Above all, they should not accept reactionary collaborators (Canon Aristide Magnier, of Soissons, or the Jesuit, Joseph Brucker).

Father Lagrange's editorial comments to Batiffol were explicit:

> Look over the chronicle of Semeria, and do not let anything suspect pass, because they have it in for him. We could lose him, and we would then seem to have launched him and then abandoned him. But, on the other hand, I beg you to include nothing in the line of Magnier and Brucker. I believe that Mgr. d'Hulst has exaggerated in his description of the broad school, but the truth is not far from it. We need to declare ourselves boldly for the broad opinion, then give it some boundaries and render it theological. I would like to do this, but I feel that I would break myself in the attempt. Let us wait. But nothing of Magnier!

The authorities of the order kept watch over every article, limiting freedom of expression. All the articles written by Father Lagrange—at least on disputed questions—had to be submitted to a Roman censorship, imposed in October 1893, and worsened in September 1899, and which would become more and more constraining, more and more fanatical. Meanwhile, despite the shackles to which Father Lagrange submitted, the *Revue biblique* opened a breach in the wall separating Catholics from others.

"As regards the *Revue biblique*, the result that I sought is attained. If they find my tendencies dangerous, I only ask that I remain silent, in spite of my intimate conviction that we are on the right road," he wrote on January 28, 1895. "The mail that I have found here shows me more and more to what extent we are favorably viewed in the Protestant world. Of course, I recognize that that makes our role very delicate, but is it not something to see it recognized in scholarly journals in France, in England, in Germany, that we are working with competence and with perfect honesty, yet all the while subject to the church? Cannot that do them some good? They have reproached us so much for neglecting the Bible," he wrote on March 21, 1896. "Many minds are being opened. The program realized is immense, and it is a consolation for me to think that it is in great measure due to the *Revue biblique*" reads his entry from May 29, 1899.

At the end of seven years of an agitated existence due to polemics aroused by the adversaries of the *Revue biblique*, "the reactionary party does not disarm," wrote Father Lagrange on May 29, 1899. In Paris, some Dominicans forbade their penitents to read the *Revue*. In Jerusalem, the *Revue* was outlawed in certain communities. At the Assumptionists', the superior general forbade its reading and prohibited the order's young religious from attending courses at the École biblique. At the White Fathers', an order came from on high: "Continue to receive the *Revue* so as not to offend the Dominicans, but do not allow it to circulate within the community, where it could not do any good." The superior of the Betharram Fathers then declared: "There are some professors of the holy scripture who, if they would meet Father Lagrange in a corner, would perhaps dust him up." Nevertheless, the success achieved by the *Revue biblique* in seven years was incontestable, even though Father Lagrange held firm to his resolution of not pleasing his public by making it easy for them. The *Revue biblique*, at the end of 1898, reached a circulation of 836 copies, and progress still continued during the following years. The list of subscribers at that moment testifies to the breakthrough in the French Catholic world that the *Revue* had already effected. Two-thirds of the seminaries were receiving it. Among the clergy, those that one can call the "simple priests" (pastors, associates, chaplains), who subscribed through personal interest and not because of their function, constituted 19.7 percent of paying subscribers. More surprising still, 12 percent of the subscribers were country pastors, scattered in forty-nine departments of rural France where one would not expect to find so much interest in the progress of biblical exegesis. Father Lagrange had wanted to give back the taste for strong studies to the clergy. The objective was beginning to be attained.

By 1902, an audience outside the Catholic Church had been attained. Solomon Reinach, in a report in the *Revue Critique d'histore et de littératuer*, recognized that the *Revue biblique* had become, in only a few years, the most important organ of well-informed exegesis. "It is the Catholics, above all, who are interested in knowing which movements in different directions are being produced in Protestant criticism. There is no better way to know how times have changed. Ignorance and lack of curiosity are not fashionable any more; that is why the criticism called Protestant penetrates into the Catholic milieu. Before, they vilified it without explaining; today, they explain it without making a duty of it always to vilify. This is a serious gain for scientific honesty in general and for biblical studies in particular."

Scarcely five years after the birth of the *Revue biblique*, Father Lagrange, envisioned another wave of scholarly publications, a *Library of Theological Education*. His sweeping proposal would be reduced to a series: *Études bibliques*. On February 2, 1897, he modestly proposed the plan to the master of the order:

> I come to ask for your decision and your blessing for a project on which I have long reflected. It is already several years that I have been teaching holy scripture, and

still I have a lot to learn. That is due to many reasons, among others, because I started a little late. However that may be, I am no longer young [he was 42 years old], and I feel that I must put in order the little knowledge that I have acquired.

I ask myself if it would be useful, today, since my classes no longer demand so much preparation, since the *Revue biblique* has caught on so well, to begin a more complete work, more ordered than unrelated articles. This would not be ready for three or four years, but I do not want even to begin the work without your approval. My idea would be to make a study of the Old Testament as a literary critic, a special introduction to each book, trying to determine the epoch, the character, and so forth. This would end up as a history of Israel and a theology of the Old Testament. The whole would take seven or eight years. Would the good Lord give me them? In any case, I would employ them for his glory.

Tell me what you think of this proposal; I remain in indifference. I will always have enough to do if I busy myself with the duties of my state and of my health. It is not a permission that I am asking for, it is an idea that I bring up to you faithfully, expecting that you would either tell me "don't do anything," or "go ahead." I shall understand either response as coming from God.

The authorization was only granted in a grudging manner, to judge by the note in the curia's register: "The Most Reverend Father does not oppose your plan, provided that these studies do not harm the courses and the *Revue biblique*. He expresses the wish that Father Lagrange find some dedicated collaborators." Father Lagrange moved immediately to accomplish this goal. In December 1897, the printer Protat, of Mâcon, estimated the printing costs of *Commentaries on Scripture* for Victor Lecoffre. At the beginning of 1898, Father Lagrange worked steadily to complete his Genesis commentary, from which he expected a decisive breakthrough: "The publication of such a work would be of much greater importance than articles in the *Revue biblique*." By April 1897, the work was well advanced. "My work on Genesis that you have deigned to bless," he wrote to the master of the order on April 24, "is almost finished." Writing to a Dominican in Paris the next day, Lagrange hoped that the controversy stirred up against his article on the author of the Pentateuch would calm down. "But Father Didon is right, it would take a volume. My Genesis is going to be ready, but there is, canonically, an enormous difference between all the articles in the world and a book. Let us hope. We only want the good, and we will keep quiet, if silence is best."

He did not realize how truly he had spoken. While he was dreaming of the publication of Genesis and of distributing other books of the Bible to different collaborators and of undertaking Exodus himself, the Roman censor deemed the publication of the manuscript inopportune. One of his censors explained:

> The work does not contain anything that could be reproved. But theologians are not well informed about Orientalism: That is why modern criticism frightens them more than it benefits them. That being the case, it is to be feared that they will accuse you of temerity for the abandonment of certain opinions still in favor. Criticism, however healthy and wise it may be, will not be able to triumph overnight. Some articles would better prepare public opinion, which the publication of a book would risk shocking. Whatever may be the value of the works of Father Lagrange (works which I am pleased to honor), it is necessary that they appear at the right time and not go beyond the present capacity of those that they ought to instruct.

In brief, the publication of the commentary on Genesis seemed premature. Father Lagrange, putting aside Genesis, for better days he hoped, set to work on Judges. But he did this without any further encouragement from the master of the order, who wrote him in November 1899. "Since I feel confident with you, I shall tell you frankly that a translation of the Book of Judges or any other books of the Old Testament, according to the method you indicate, would be little appreciated or would be judged badly. And my advice is that you abstain from such a work."

Meanwhile, the project of the *Études biblique* series, duly approved by the cardinal perfect and by the secretary of the Index, received authorization to appear in the *Revue biblique*, where it was published in July 1900, under the title: "Project of a Complete Commentary on Holy Scripture." The contract concerning the course on holy scripture, entitled this time, "Holy Scripture Translated and Explained According to the Original Texts and the Most Ancient Versions," is signed by M. J. Lagrange and L. H. Vincent with the publisher as V. Lecoffre, October 11, 1901. Since the series was not allowed to begin, as would have been normal, with Genesis, it started with Judges, in 1903. This was a victory won over the hesitations of the master of the order, because the publication of this volume had for a long time been questioned. Publication had been suspended in June 1900; then, in August 1900, it was judged preferable that the work appear, if not entirely in Latin, at least accompanied by the text of the Vulgate; approved by the censors in January 1902, and only authorized at that moment by the master of the order. It was still in suspense in the month of February. "These poor judges are not getting anywhere. It seems as if the father general has been retaken by terror. He always wants things that cannot be attacked! So, we re-edit! And then what? No even St. Thomas [would survive], I think, after the *Bull Ineffabilis!* This exaggerated pragmatism in doctrinal matters is strange when one arrives at it through so many concessions of all sorts. It is to want to be afraid for the fun of it, to fear a schism. But he is sure that the moment will come when they will demand a little latitude. If that is what the bureaucrats call a *schism*...the church cannot be governed like a religious order." Right up to the last moment considerations of opportuneness prevailed over those of truth. But publication of Judges seemed a harmless affair in comparison to publication of Genesis. That would carry the decision. None of the books of the Pentateuch would find a place in the *Études bibliques* series.

Other means of contacting the scholarly world presented themselves. At the Institut de France, the Académie des inscriptions et belle-lettres, which was interested in Semitic inscriptions, entrusted some missions of exploration to the École biblique. Sometimes these were not without risk, as on the trip to Petra in October 1897. Father Lagrange himself told how they had believed Father Vincent dead. He had lost his way and had not returned to the campsite by nightfall. They were already looking for his cadaver, following the flight of vultures, when he came back safe and sound. The trip home was still more perilous, because the explorers fell into an ambush during which they lost their escort as well as their baggage under a hail of bullets. Father Lagrange and Father Vincent were within two fingers' breadth of facing death in this trap. Father Lagrange recalled: "I said to Vincent, 'Let us give one another absolution.' And he began fumbling for his breviary. 'The shortest!' I cried out."

Speakers' invitations to scholarly meetings were furnishing an occasional platform from which the teaching of the École would find a broader audience than at St. Stephen. In regard to the Congress of Orientalists, held in Geneva in September 1894, where Father Lagrange had met Professor Müller, his former teacher in Vienna, and where he had presented to the Palestinologists an Armenian mosaic discovered in the excavations of St. Stephen, he concluded his report in the *Revue biblique* gracefully. "We would like to encourage, as much as we can, learned Catholics to attend these congresses. We are received there, I know, with perfect courtesy." To the master of the order, Father Lagrange explained what stimulation he had found at the congress for his own research. "I was very well received, but I noted again how much we have to do to equal these scholars. That has given me courage, and I need it, because I am profoundly sad to see how little the governing bodies of the order understand our work, useful to all. I am becoming odious to many persons in the order, who would be very attached to me if I had remained tranquil in my province."

With the idea of climbing over the walls behind which Catholics took cover and engaging in dialogue with other specialists in biblical sciences, the inventive mind of Father Lagrange conceived another project less indirect. Father Lagrange spoke of it to the master of the order in August 1897, on returning from the Congress of Fribourg, where the position of the École on the Pentateuch had found favorable reception.

> The success of Fribourg confirms me in an idea that I have thought about for a long time: to try to penetrate the secular University of Paris, so that Catholic teaching can gain a forceful hearing there. Perhaps in asking only to offer some free courses, one would obtain permission to speak, without expecting honorariums. Intelligent young people do not come and will not come to look for us in our convents; we need to go to them. We need to take back our place in the sun, in the full light of day. It is not enough for Dominicans to edify some women in their chapels. We need to tackle a broad scholarly discussion on the topic. I submit this idea to your Paternity. It is completely identical to what Berthier thought.

The response was foreseeable: "The plan of trying to introduce Catholic teaching to the University of France by giving some free courses there seems scarcely realizable, at least for the moment. Reverend Father had better continue his dedication to the serious work in Jerusalem, where one cannot replace him for the moment."

It was then from Jerusalem, through the channel of the *Revue biblique* and the *Études bibliques* that Father Lagrange would have to reach the learned public. But he did not resign himself to seeing the Dominicans absent from the Parisian university environment. To Ambroise Gardeil, whom he regretted having missed in Paris, he confided in October 1898: "I would have told you of my increasing desire to see you established in Paris and making an opening in the university. That is the future....The Sulpicians, for a long time held back by M. Icard, are spreading all over, becoming professionals in theology, the intellectual masters of the clergy by two steps, while our teaching without echo is given in the villages. In ten years, will it be time to reconquer this lost terrain, or is our role in this sense finished?" Less than ten years later, the Saulchoir, directed by Ambroise Gardeil, would create in its turn the *Revue des sciences philosophiques et theologiques* in 1907.

In the intention of Father Lagrange, the École biblique of Jerusalem is a Dominican apostolic work. Through its service of truth, its work for the salvation of souls, it fulfills the goals of the Order of Preachers. "We don't want souls to be lost for refusing adherence to what the church does not ask them to believe," concluded Father Lagrange in 1897, at the end of an article on the story of the Fall in Genesis. If his language is sometimes a bit antiquated, a little stuffy, more like the style of Thérèse of Lisieux his contemporary than that of Duchesne or of Loisy (even though, in polemic, his pen is sometimes stinging), the clarity and the firmness of his plan do not leave anything to be desired, nor does his untiring perseverance against winds and tides, combined with the most sincere submission. Father Lagrange is not an arrogant challenger: He is the humble servant, obeying and praying.

Chapter IV

THE STRUGGLES
OF FATHER LAGRANGE:
THE FRIBOURG CONGRESS (1897)

Father Lagrange often received word from his Roman superiors advising him to confine himself to defensive tactics in his scholarly pursuits: Lock the doors to the church; let those outside the church carry on the struggle. While he waited for a scholarly consensus to form through other scholars' works, he was warned to limit himself to occasional remarks. Father Lagrange asked himself, "Is this how we really serve the truth or the people who risk getting lost in the meantime? Would it not be better to endanger my peace and even my reputation than to be silent out of a carnal prudence?" Rather than keeping out of the struggle, bemoaning the circumstances, or retreating from criticism, Father Lagrange preferred to throw himself into the fight. Criticism was his most effective weapon: "Only criticism can cure the evil caused by criticism." He assured the master of the order, "The École biblique is the highest intellectual enterprise capable of seizing the weapon of criticism from the unbelievers and the Protestants in the domain of scripture." Scholarly honesty demanded not a defensive strategy but an offensive one. Father Lagrange came up with an aggressive strategy for determining the authenticity of shrines, one that would be just as valid if applied to interpretations of scripture. "The great interest of the church is that we be enough enamored of the truth to demolish by ourselves the certainly false traditions, while at the same time upholding the true ones."

What about the literary composition of Genesis? Is Moses the author of the Pentateuch, the first five books of the Bible? These questions were not the least serious or the least urgent of those that criticism had raised. Father Lagrange decided to seize the occasion of the Congress of Fribourg in 1897 to take a public stand on these contentious issues.

The creation of the International Scientific Congresses of Catholics had been suggested by Canon Duilhé de Saint-Projet to Bishop d'Hulst, who was to become the mainspring of the movement. The purpose of the congresses was twofold. They would encourage the exchange of information and ideas among Catholic scholars working in very varied fields, and they would also enable theologians to listen to the words of responsible experts in exact sciences as well as in historical criticism. They were interdisciplinary. Successive congresses were held in Paris (1888 and 1891), Brussels (1894), Fribourg (1897), and Munich (1900). The sixth congress, planned for Rome in 1903, was not able to convene: By then the circumstances were no longer favorable for this kind of forum. The success these congresses enjoyed is difficult to imagine today. The Congress of Fribourg brought together for four days, August 16 to August 20, more than three-thousand participants. Two-hundred forum papers were published in *Acts*, a congress publication comprising approximately two-thousand pages. On the occasion of the congress of 1897, the organizing committee, pushed by Father Batiffol, had divided Section I, Religious Sciences, and created Section II, Exegetical Sciences. The new orientation personified by Father Lagrange would show itself there in strength. Of the twenty papers presented, four were by Dominicans (Lagrange, Rose, Schiel, Séjourné), and five others were by contributors to the *Revue biblique* or by friends of the School of Jerusalem (Batiffol, Calmes, Ermoni, Germer-Durand, Minocchi).

Lagrange had been associated with the preparation of the Congress and had proposed a contribution on the sources of Genesis. His paper had been announced in the *Revue biblique* in April 1897. In fact, the paper would treat, in a more global manner, the Mosaic authenticity of the Pentateuch, a particularly burning point, on which the scholarly comparison of the text with the land itself had brought some enlightenment. The archaeological trip carried out by the École biblique in the Sinai, from February to March 1896, had sometimes confirmed, sometimes changed the reading of Exodus, and thus the Pentateuch. "In my mind, it developed like a spiritual discernment in a complicated matter; it seemed to me that the terrain itself had a word to say on [the historicity of some details] of the Pentateuch." The distinguishing of the literary sources, examined on the sites of the Exodus, confirmed the reality of the stories more than it weakened them. But it was necessary to recognize that the style the Bible employed was foreign to the historical practice codified by Langlois and Seignobos. (Their *Introduction to Historical Studies* is dated 1897.) Biblical historiography belongs to a cultural world which the Positivist historiography of the nineteenth century did not take into account. "[We aim] to set down the principle of a certain style of writing history which is not our own but which is found in the Old Testament."

On March 15, 1897, one year after Father Lagrange's firsthand experience on the land, at the moment when he was developing his paper for the Fribourg Congress, he revealed his preoccupation to the master of the order. "I believe myself obliged to renounce the Mosaic authenticity of the Pentateuch, as an edited whole, and I believe that it is on this ground that one can most effectively defend the supernatural intervention of God in the history of Israel. I have hesitated for a long time to do it openly, although it has been my conviction for a long time, but I believe that the same movement is becoming more pronounced from various sides of the Catholic world." At that point, Father Lagrange did not know that on January 13, an intimidating salvo had been fired from Rome by the Holy Office in the direction of the exegetes who were planning to contribute to the Congress of Fribourg. It was the decree of the Supreme Congregation of the Holy Roman and Universal Inquisition (January 13, 1897), which did not reach Jerusalem until April 9. The decree maintained the authenticity of chapter 5, verse 7, of the First Epistle of John, as it figures in the Vulgate. "There are three who testify in *heaven: the Father, the Word, and the Holy Spirit, and these three are one; and there are three which testify on earth:* the spirit, the water, and the blood, and these three are one." The Holy Office enjoined the professional exegetes to read the later additions to the text (in italics) as just as "authorized" as the rest of the Bible. Communicating this decree to Father Lagrange, Father Granello, commissar of the Holy Office, said that it was directed "against the excesses of a certain school of criticism" toward which certain authors published in the *Revue biblique* had shown themselves a bit too favorable.

The first response of Father Lagrange to the decree is lost, but the letter which he addressed to the master of the order on April 11 suggests the tenor of his former letter:

Most Reverend Father:

It was in a state of confusion and in a moment of discouragement that I wrote my last letter to you. I entreat you to excuse me and ask you not to pay attention to it, except in order to impose a penance upon me, which I have well earned. I ask only the favor of being admitted to the blessings of the Dominican life, no matter where, and in the position that you see fit to place me. I believe that I can say, however, that my intentions in teaching have always been pure. I understand and admire this attachment to the church that makes one unwilling to differ from the most common opinions. But it seems to me that I have seen in St. Jerome another sort of attachment that sustained him in all his labors, the desire to see the church triumph over her adversaries. It is truly a passion which devours me: this regret about not finding all of the forces in us Catholics that I would like to find, about seeing the church mocked by some powerful enemies, as in the days of St. Jerome when some Jews reproached him for the inferiority of his version!

Finally, I would deeply like a strong, armed, powerful Catholic exegesis, but this seems impossible to me without a certain freedom of discussion that would allow us to put the best arms of our enemies to use in the service of faith.

I live for nothing else, but I possess a blind faith in obedience. And if I am convinced through study that the system which I advocate will lead to the destruction of Protestantism and to the glory of the church, I know also that in the Catholic Church, all should be subject to the principle of authority. If the time has not yet come, I will wait, and it will only be time for me when I have the full consent of my superiors.

Do then all you deem right in my regard, Father. I wait on bent knees to receive your orders. Deign only to bless me, to recommend me to our Lord, and to accept this expression of my profound respect and my perfect obedience.

Father Lagrange was faced with a hard decision. Should he attend the conference in Fribourg himself, or should he have another member of the congress read his paper? "Will you be at the Fribourg Congress?" he asked Henry Hyvernat, on May 1. "I do not yet know whether Father General is going to send me there. As for myself, I have made the firm decision not to make a request to attend." In fact, Father Lagrange did not count on going to France during the summer of 1897. He requested permission only belatedly. "Having been in France during my last vacation," he wrote to the master of the order on June 27, "I promised myself that I would not ask if I could make the trip again this year; however, the prior thinks that this trip would be justified by the Catholic Congress in Fribourg and by the Congress of Orientalists in Paris. Indeed, perhaps we would be able to meet students there, or at least be able to meet some adherents of the work of our school and of the *Revue*. If you judge this trip to be well timed, I will go to France following the final exams, which will be held on July 17."

The ensuing trip to France allowed Father Lagrange to be near his ill mother, Élisabeth, in Bourg-en-Bresse. From there, on August 6, he requested to meet the master of the order at the Dominican house of Oullins. To fulfill the desire of the master, the prepared paper was submitted to two censors of the order, Father Berthier and Father Gardeil, who gave their support. Thus, Lagrange did not risk his all without surrounding himself with a safety net of guarantees.

The paper, prepared with such care by Father Lagrange, was not presented as a lesson in exegesis or explanation as was von Hügel's paper. Instead, Father Lagrange's paper was centered on one prejudicial question: "Are the reasons for which Catholics have been, up until now, hindered from tackling an examination of the Pentateuch decisive?"

Father Lagrange summarized the five reasons most often given in support of the authenticity of the Pentateuch in order to argue their decisiveness:

1. The editing of the holy books has been a continuous string of additions: Nothing obliges one to attribute the final state of the text to Moses.

2. The Bible contains several successive law codes, which show a progressive evolution, all placed under Moses' authority: Moses is not, for all that, the final editor.

3. The passages in the Old and New Testaments, which refer to Moses, attribute to him a story or a sentence: They do not in any way prove that Moses edited the Pentateuch.

4. The historical tradition concerning the role allotted to Moses in God's plan is part of our faith; whereas, the literary tradition concerning the writings attributed to Moses do not at all enjoy the same authority.

5. The historical value of the biblical accounts ought to be judged not by our scientific and positivist manner of understanding history but ought to be judged by the use to which the people of the Bible put the story.

Rather than delve into a dissection of the Pentateuch and of the documents on which "the work of Moses" is constituted, Father Lagrange, responding to the formalized question, set forth the theological hermeneutics, or scientific interpretation, of the Bible. Simply put, Father Lagrange suggested that the religious authority of the Bible is not based upon the literary *authenticity* of the writings of Moses, David, Isaiah, Solomon, or others but upon the *divine inspiration* of the editors of the text as it was received by the church. It would be necessary, however, to wait for the conciliar constitution *Dei Verbum*, promulgated on November 18, 1965, to break the link between inspiration and authenticity in church documents. The divine guarantee bears on the history of salvation, the plan of which is revealed by God's Word. It does not bear on the historicity of biblical stories. This requires other criteria for reading. Few of Father Lagrange's Catholic contemporaries were ready or willing to understand, much less to adopt, these principles.

During the congress, however, Father Lagrange's conspicuous intervention did not provoke the confrontation with theologians that he had feared. Even the Jesuit Father Brucker, who would become more and more critical in *Études* as time passed, proved conciliatory. According to one published account, "Father Brucker, without sharing all of the author's conclusions, states that research such as this can be very useful to Catholic scholarship. He believes that there is no reason for a Catholic to deny the diversity of the sources." Father Lagrange himself was satisfied: "I was happy to find myself in perfect affinity with them (Berthier and Gardeil) and with the other theologians of our order. They understand well that I hold to philosophical and theological principles as much as they do. I believe that our place in the sun is assured; all that is needed now is to avoid imprudence, while serving the cause of truth without too much opportunism."

The time of tolerant goodwill was passing rapidly. Before long, the harshest controversy would erupt. At the turn of the century, however, an immense field was open to criticism, not only of holy scripture but also of church history. Criticism might be leveled at Christian origins; the supposedly apostolic origin of the churches of France was the object of a lively controversy. Pious traditions, such as the authenticity of the Holy Land shrines founded by crusaders, or the specific locations of biblical episodes, did not go unchallenged. Even the authenticity of venerable relics were questioned, the Holy Shroud of Turin and the Holy House of Loretto, for instance. In short, Duchesne, the Bollandists, and the École biblique were all engaged in the same struggle. Before them lay a growing united front. A new wave of popular fundamentalism had begun to rise, reaching even the higher clergy. Enlightenment was being extinguished, and a simpleminded credulity prevailed. The clergy blindly accepted the ramblings of Diana Vaughan, a pseudomystic created by Leo Taxil and unveiled by him as a hoax on April 19, 1897. Still, they foolishly refused to allow the application of historical criticism in the religious domain.

Under these conditions, publishing the paper given at the Congress of Fribourg in the *Revue biblique* required a courageous decision. Father Vigouroux advised against it. Father Batiffol encouraged it. The article could not fail to appear as the manifesto of the École Biblique. It would be seen as a rallying flag for the innovators, as well as for the moderates. It would not be long before it would serve as a target for conservatives. "*Sciens et prudens, manum misi in ignem*: Fully cognizant of the situation, following St. Jerome, I plunge my hand into the fire," stated Father Lagrange. He preferred the struggle for the Bible, in which blows rained down heavily, to a contemplative Orientalism that would earn him consideration and honors. "I am convinced that there is a campaign to continue," Father Lagrange wrote to the master of the order in 1898, "where there will be many nuisances to endure, prejudices to overcome, and attacks to withstand patiently. Why not remain serenely on the beaten path? Because I am passionately taken with the honor of the church and because it seems to me that it works for the good of souls."

The article, entitled "The Sources of the Pentateuch," appeared prominently in the *Revue biblique* of January 1898. Reactions varied. In Rome Father Genocchi, professor of exegesis at the Apollinare, and Cardinal Parocchi, vicar of Rome, expressed their admiration. Father Eschbach, superior of the French seminary in Rome, did not hide his displeasure. In Paris, on January 20, *L'univers* opened fire through an article by Reverend Barbin. The article itself would not have merited much attention, if not for the fact that it unleashed the inquisitorial zeal of the patriarch of Jerusalem. The year finished with a severe charge by Father Lucien Mechineau, in the *Études* of November 5. Even worse than the hostilities in the press were the hostilities of the clergy itself. Patriarch Piavi denounced Father Lagrange to Cardinal Ledochowski, prefect of Propaganda, who was already strongly prejudiced against the École biblique: "We have to destroy this nest of heresies," he responded. Father Ledochowski handed the file over to the Holy Office. In Rome, everything was known: The rumor circulated that grave sanctions were about to descend upon Father Lagrange. He wrote on May 28 to the master of the order:

> I understand very well that the operations of the Congregation of the Holy Office are secret; however, if I knew on which points the criticisms of me are based, perhaps it would be easier for me to explain myself....In any case, my most Reverend Father, let my person not be an obstacle. If it is enough for the Sacred Congregation that you reprimand me and call me back to France, noting well that you may take the direction of the school away from me, do it without fearing the slightest sign of discontent on my part. I admit that I desire with all my soul that the Congregation not

notice anything, prohibit anything, or condemn anything, and it seems to me that this is less for myself than for the honor of the church. I tell you these things as I see them. If I were condemned, I would submit, but since I have not been and since I hope not to be, I believe myself to have been in the truth. I fear that the good souls will make a decision like the one on the three witnesses that had to be toned down soon afterward. It would be better to take me away, and perhaps then, the school of St. Étienne, relieved of my person, would only operate better.

Even though the examination of the file against Father Lagrange remained in suspense, his friend Father Genocchi, guilty of having presented to the Italian Society for Biblical Studies, on February 10, a report on the current state of criticism regarding the Pentateuch, witnessed the hatchet beginning its descent. Meanwhile, Father Lagrange persuaded himself that the case might have been dismissed because no grounds for prosecution could be found. His hopes were dashed. In May, the Society for Biblical Studies was abolished. In June, the chair of exegesis at the Apollinare was abolished. In the February issue of the *Échos d'Orient*, an article by P. Siméon Vailhé, which offered several audacious criticisms, caused a serious backlash among the Assumptionists. The author had been a member of the group of young students at Notre Dame de France who had been sent to take courses on holy scripture at St. Étienne. The juvenile audacity of Father Vailhé had been blamed on Father Lagrange by the patriarch of Jerusalem, as well as by the superiors of the congregation. "The school of St. Étienne," explained Father Emmanuel Bailly, "has done us a serious wrong, one of the most grievous wounds that an institute which is just being born could possibly sustain. Father Lagrange denies having taught this or that to our young people, but he has allowed the spirit of intellectual independence to infiltrate them, a spirit that led them to this or that.

Thus, in Rome, they are profoundly discontent with the movement." The incident consummated the break between the Assumptionists of Notre Dame de France and the Dominicans of St. Étienne.

Participation in the Congress of Fribourg held two important lessons for Father Lagrange. First of all, it reinforced in him the conviction that the most serious and most urgent intellectual debates are played out more in the world of the universities than in the ecclesiastical world. Second, it revealed to him that it would be necessary for him to be present there at all costs, if not through the spoken word, then at least through publications.

Father Lagrange now perceived how much the search for new solutions to the biblical crisis demanded a climate of freedom. Defense reflexes inspired by fear do not solve any scholarly difficulty. "To proceed always through coercion is to wound the intellectual vitality of the church. Is it not better to give the floor to moderate opinions, albeit a bit new?" In good faith, Father Lagrange could not abandon a struggle in which the stakes were the salvation of souls. "It seems that the moment has arrived," he declared in his paper, "when one can no longer remain in a state of inaction without compromising the salvation of souls, without alienating from the church the intellectual forces that are attached to it. It seems that in moving forward, one can win many others."

The congress confirmed Father Lagrange's competence and the authority of the École biblique. The objective of making the school known in the international scholarly community had been attained. When a calm arose at the end of the pontificate of Leo XIII, acts of confidence were not lacking. Father Lagrange was named consultor of the new Biblical Commission; the *Revue biblique* was chosen to become the organ of the Commission; a biblical institute proposed by the pope, whose realization would have been entrusted to the director of the school of Jerusalem. The death of the pope on July 20, 1903, however, effectively buried the project nurtured jointly by him and by Cardinal Rampolla.

Chapter V

THE STRUGGLES
OF FATHER LAGRANGE:
THE TOULOUSE LECTURES (1902)

The last few years of Pope Leo XIII's pontificate had been marked by a sharp turn from the reprimand addressed to the Franciscan friars in November 1888 to the support shown in the creation of the Biblical Commission in August 1901. The commission was realized in October 1902. The death in March 1900 of the Jesuit Cardinal Mazzella, whose support for the most conservative positions had, up until then, been decisive, probably had something to do with this sudden change of course.

Pope Leo XIII's letter to the Franciscan minister general in 1888 had reproached his order: "Even those who should have been least susceptible thought they could adopt in biblical exegesis a type of interpretation which was too bold and free." The man who was most directly targeted was Father David Fleming. Father Fleming was then teaching holy scripture at St. Anthony College in Rome, where he was denounced by his own brethren for the boldness of his teaching. There were also quite a few malevolent interpreters who were only too glad to apply the pope's warning against the new exegesis to Father Lagrange's work. Such criticism would have been understandable had it come from the Jesuit Fathers Mechineau or Brucker in *Études;* they were always willing to use any means to serve their cause. Much of the criticism was coming from the Dominican Order itself, however. The prior of St. Étienne, writing to Father Xavier Faucher on December 19, said: "The second part of this letter is obviously aimed at us. Its terms are serious. Father Lagrange must absolutely be much more careful. In fact, he must have felt this criticism since he gave up his intention of publishing an article on the Flood in the *Revue*, which, I fear, would have raised new storms. Without going deeply into the matter, we must admit that his opinions cannot but cause some astonishment and some alarm, at least at first."

On January 28, 1899, the master general's attitude did not differ from the prior's attitude. "The Most Reverend Father reminds Father Lagrange that he must not publish his work on the Pentateuch without authorizations nor translate his article on the "Origins of the Pentateuch" for *Rassegna nazionale* and insists that he should follow, point by point, the advice given to the Franciscans by the Supreme Pontiff." This letter put more stress on the warning to the Franciscans than did the former note, which is registered in the Ledger of the Curia, dated January 25. The master general was not keen to draw fire from the Holy See. "My intention, as I make these remarks to you, is that you make the warnings given by the Supreme Pontiff to the Franciscans your own. You must do your best to ensure that nothing, in the courses and scholastic exercises…given in your school or in public lectures or in the articles published in the *Revue biblique*, might be thought contrary to the teachings of the Holy Father."

The master general now gave stricter orders for the control of the *Revue biblique*. None of Father Lagrange's articles were to be published without the endorsement of designated censors.

> The Reverend Father General has appointed the Reverend Father Thomas Esser, 41 via Condotti, Rome, and the Reverend Father Master Reginald Walsh, professor at Maynooth College near Dublin, Ireland, examiners of Father Lagrange's articles for the *Revue biblique*. Two examiners, chosen from the following [list], shall examine articles contributed by all others: the Reverend Fathers Monsabre, Villard, Gardeil,

Schwalm, Hurtaud and Sertillanges. The editor, or rather the secretary [Sertillanges], must be extremely cautious and ready to set aside any article that might not comply with the traditional interpretation and that might be considered an innovation.

Neither was the letter "Depuis le jour," sent by Pope Leo XIII to the French clergy on September 8, 1899, of a kind that would put Father Lagrange's mind at ease. The directives the professors of holy scripture were to follow with their students were anything but liberal.

They should especially warn them against some disturbing tendencies that seek to infiltrate interpretations of the Bible and that, were they to prevail, would soon ruin its inspiration and its supernatural character. Under the specious pretext of taking away from the enemies of the revealed Word the use of seemingly irrefutable arguments against the authenticity and the veracity of holy scripture, some Catholic writers have thought it clever of themselves to make these arguments their own. Because of this strange and dangerous tactic, they have, with their own hands, helped to open gaps in the wall of the city that it was their duty to defend....We have put an end to this dangerous rashness.

The mistrust of his superiors weighed upon Father Lagrange. On November 26, 1899, he wrote: "I have every reason for feeling discouraged. From Rome, I receive nothing reassuring. They are always afraid of my imprudence." Yet, he felt sure of the course the school should follow. "The real future of the [Dominican] house is the biblical school," he explained to the general curia on July 3, 1901. "It has had the brakes put on it for a time and has gone through a crisis, for various reasons, mostly, if you like, because of the doctrinal line I have taken. I expected as much. *Sciens et prudens misi manum in ignem*: It is easy to get the applause of an incompetent public if you adopt a routine stance. I preferred a scholarly approach, a progressive exegesis that was sure to be that of the future. I believe it is now clear that I was not mistaken."

At the turn of the century, an unexpected change in policy took place in Rome. Coming from the Holy See, the idea of creating a commission devoted to biblical questions, which had up until then been subject to the Holy Office and to the Congregation for the Index, meant a step forward. Pressing, delicate problems would be examined by competent men whose mission would lie more in promoting than in checking biblical studies. The new commission (or "small commission," to distinguish it from the "great commission" of October 1900) was set up in August 1901, made public in December, and started its work in January 1902. It was modeled on the larger Roman Congregation with two levels of authority, one for consultation and one for deliberation. The twelve consultors were chosen for having been neither denouncers nor accusers. Most were considered liberal. No notorious opponents of the new exegesis were included. As to the cardinals, the chairman, Lucido Maria Parocchi, was considered open-minded. His death in January 1902 would be considered prejudicial to the progress of biblical research. The two other cardinals, Francesco Segna, and especially Jose Calasanz Vives y Tuto, were known for their conservatism.

The new Biblical Commission had obviously been created to erase the bad memories left by the decree of the Holy Office regarding the "three heavenly witnesses." "The formation of the Roman Commission," wrote Father Lagrange to the Jesuit Albert Condamin, on January 27, 1902, "appears to me a great good. Exegesis is the only science in which everyone considers himself competent...to judge without special studies and to dispute every point without consulting those who spend their lives at this hard task. Let us hope that it will not be like that anymore." A few days later, in the same mood, he wrote to Father Xavier Faucher: "We can begin to feel safer. If, indeed, Father Poels is a member of the commission, as writes *L' univers*, it is comprised of the men who were persecuted only yesterday! You must appreciate the evolution.

So, the most important thing to do hereafter is to hold back those who are impatient and not to do anything reckless. For this, we must have technicians. Speechifying will not remedy the situation, although speeches can help to give a certain direction."

Father Lagrange had not been called to be a member of the new commission, but his advice could be heard through the voice of the secretary for the Index, the Dominican Father Thomas Esser. Father Esser wrote to Father Lagrange; "I will always turn to you for all the questions for which I am not competent, and I hope that, in the interest of the holy cause, you will not refuse me your insights and your high and eminent competence. Do take heart. Your efforts will not be wasted, and they will be acknowledged and appreciated by the church itself. Santa Patienza!"

When the Biblical Commission was expanded to include five cardinals and forty consultants and definitively constituted on October 1902 by the apostolic letter, *Vigilantiae*, Father Lagrange was soon nominated as a consultor (January 26, 1903). The master general was glad to see in this nomination the rehabilitation of the founder of the École biblique. He wrote: "The satisfaction I feel is the greater as such a result could hardly have been expected after the crisis we went through some years ago and which was so painful for me and you. The sorrow and grief your Paternity had to suffer during those days, and which I shared, with their trail of worries and distressing torments, appear well compensated, in my eyes, by this act of the Holy Father. By the same blow, he has put an end to the accusations made by adversaries of honesty. Thank God for it!"

Simultaneous to the struggle that ended in the establishment of the Biblical Commission, a second public struggle involving the propriety of a series of public lectures at Toulouse was being carried on by the director of the École biblique. Father Lagrange delivered the Toulouse lectures on historical method in November 1902, without prior critical review. Conservatives raised a furor about their propriety and attempted to block their publication. The lectures were published in March 1903.

Had it not been for the friendship between Father Lagrange and Father Batiffol, dating back to their time at the Issy seminary, there would never have been a series of lectures in Toulouse at all. From the beginning, Father Batiffol had collaborated with Father Lagrange. Writings by Father Batiffol had appeared in the *Revue biblique* as early as 1892. In 1895, having become a subeditor for the *Revue*, he gave the publication the clear layout it was to keep ever after. In February 1898, having been approached about becoming the rector of the Catholic University of Toulouse, Father Batiffol saw in his new responsibility the chance to collaborate with Father Lagrange in Toulouse. "If I go to Toulouse, my first visit will be to your provincial and, in agreement with the archbishop, to ask for you. We shall organize a faculty of theology. The Jesuits will have Paris to do as they please. As for us two, we shall both keep on with our agreement on a new basis." Father Batiffol's proposal was not accepted enthusiastically. The master general firmly refused all requests to have Father Lagrange come to Toulouse, in 1898, in 1900, and again in 1901. After all, what would happen to the École biblique without Father Lagrange? There was no understudy trained to step into his role. Although Father Lagrange was tempted by the project, he noted in his *Personal Reflections and Memoirs*: "To go to Toulouse, which did not offer the advantages of Paris, would have been desertion."

On the other hand, the influence that Father Batiffol had had on the *Revue biblique* constituted one of the grievances against Father Lagrange. In fact, Father Lagrange was obliged to dismiss his subeditor on the pretext that he could not be both rector of Toulouse and subeditor of the *Revue*. "Please remember," wrote Father Lagrange to the master general in March 1902, "that it was on your express order that I deprived myself of Monsignor Batiffol's help, he who at the time used to do as much, or perhaps more, than I did for the *Revue biblique*. Since then he has grown cooler. This is understandable, since I had to ask him to resign. On this occasion, as in many others, my courage was sorely tried. But during a retreat, I made the resolution always to carry on, to perform a humble and faithful service, as long as the master general does not reduce me to the kind of impotence that would amount to a disavowal."

At last, it seemed the two friends were going to have the opportunity to work together again. The new *Bulletin de litterature écclesiastique*, created in 1899 in Toulouse by Father Batiffol, was to be published in coordination with the *Revue biblique*. The two scholars would collaborate on both publications. Father Batiffol contributed regularly to the *Revue* until 1920, but Father Lagrange, who wrote a third of the *Revue biblique*, contributed to the *Bulletin* only once, in 1899.

When Father Batiffol invited Father Lagrange to give a few public lectures at the Catholic Institute, his intention was to further develop the collaboration between Jerusalem and Toulouse. In 1901, the general master met the first invitation with reserve. He outlined his objections in a letter to the prior of St. Étienne on August 29, 1901. "Given the government's policy against religious orders, is the time right to place a Dominican at the institute, while even the reigning officials there are trying not to appear as religious because of the recent laws? From whom does the invitation come? From the rector of the institute or the archbishop of Toulouse?...And what subject would be treated in these lectures?" The master general wanted to make sure that the archbishop saw nothing inconvenient in the presence of Father Lagrange. The lectures, he was assured, were to have the same subject as the book Father Lagrange was working on, which would be published in 1903 as *Studies on Semitic Religions*.

Given the master general's reluctance, Father Lagrange declined Father Batiffol's invitation. "The Reverend Prior of Jerusalem [Séjourné] wrote to ask your permission for me to give lectures at the Catholic Institute of Toulouse on the religions of the Semites. You have not written me about this, but, according to your letter to Father Séjourné, I conclude that you do not agree. Therefore, I would not think of spending October and November in Toulouse; however, Monsignor Batiffol and the Very Reverend Provincial who invited me might not understand this situation."

The opportunity missed in 1901 was offered again in 1902. According to Father Vincent's version, perhaps based on documents that have since disappeared but more probably were reconstructed long after the event, the following occurred. In the spring of 1902, Father Batiffol invited Father Lagrange to set forth the principles of his exegetical method. "His intention was that these lectures would succeed in giving the large audience of the Catholic Institute clear information about the character of his brand of progressive exegesis that too many people persisted in thinking was only a clever camouflage for Loisy's more and more alarming exegesis." Father Lagrange would probably have asked Father Batiffol to obtain, in his own name, the assent of the master general. The outline and the elements of the lectures were to have been drawn up in Jerusalem before his departure for France. According to Father Vincent, "A few days after the examinations and the end of the school year, having finished his huge manuscript on Semitic religions, Father Lagrange began immediately to write out the outline of his lectures on the historical method and intended to pull together material for them during the following weeks while he was preparing to sail to France at the beginning of August."

The documents, which still exist and can be checked in the Ledger of the General Curia, do not seem to confirm the chronology reported by Father Vincent. Because of the death of Father Lagrange's mother, Élisabeth, on May 10, the master general gave permission on June 1 for Father Lagrange to travel to France for the summer. If the ledger bears no mention of lectures to be given, that is because the trip had quite different motives. Father Lagrange, kept in Jerusalem by examinations, did not leave before July 22. It is most likely that he traveled directly to his family home in Bourg-en-Bresse. On August 22, writing from Paris, he submitted a series of questions to the master general about the state of studies at St. Étienne, about the publication of his book on Semitic religions and his commentary on Judges, and about the lectures in Toulouse.

> This project had been postponed rather than rejected last year when I did not use your kind permission to stay in France until December. Monsignor Batiffol still wants me to give them (the archbishop never interferes directly with the details of the Catholic Institute), the provincial of Toulouse seems to want them, and the prior of Jerusalem agrees. I am not asking for anything. I feel uncertain and have no special views about it. I only ask you to tell me if I should take the boat on October 2 to go back to Jerusalem or stay in France until the middle of the last week of November to give lectures (six) during two weeks at the Catholic Institute of Toulouse. I ask that you let me know your intentions as soon as possible so I can take the necessary measures. I cannot write out everything in advance because I first want to check out some details with the provincial in Toulouse; in case we print anything, I shall send it to Rome.

Father Lagrange had arrived in France at the end of August without knowing whether he would go on to Toulouse. As to the subject he would treat in his lectures, he had not said a word. The answer from Rome came quickly, but it did not refer to the subject either. "The Reverend Father is allowed to prolong his stay in France to give six lectures in Toulouse, providing the students in Jerusalem will not have to suffer in his absence." Having arrived in Toulouse by October, Father Lagrange immediately set to work.

On October 11, Father Lagrange wrote to the master general:

> I am in Toulouse where I am preparing the five or six biblical lectures that you have permitted me to give at the Catholic Institute. I thought I had better ask the Father Provincial to give me two examiners, so as not to run the risk of saying things he might not like, in his

own province. He has nominated two masters in theology, the Reverend Father Paban, who is regent, and Father Coconnier, the director of the *Revue thomiste*. This review is for the lectures, as they will be given. I write out everything, without ever being sure I shall say every word, but it is the manuscript that will count as official. The rest can be put down to the live contact with the audience or to some misunderstanding! The prior of Jerusalem urges me to publish these lectures. Will you allow me to do so, in case I find they have produced a good impression? In that case, will you be satisfied with the judgment of the two examiners in Toulouse, or must I send the manuscript to Rome? This procedure leads to a large number of copies! According to my findings, they corroborated one another: *Funiculus triplex difficile rumpitur* (Eccl 4:13).

In a postscript he added: "I am really longing to go back to Jerusalem. The institute opens its doors on November 4. I plan to give the lectures in six days and leave on the twelfth, in the evening, so as to board on the thirteenth, without even waiting for Father Lacordaire's celebration on the thirteenth, which would set me back a fortnight."

The lectures in Toulouse, though they represented twelve years of research, still appeared to be somewhat improvised. They were neither scientific communications to a congress of specialists nor a systematic course for a university audience. Father Lagrange gave them as simple talks, without scholarly footnotes, for a cultivated public who wanted to know something about the state of biblical studies. Some of the audience (perhaps the clerical group) soon showed a certain reluctance, which the archbishop tried to alleviate by presiding at the fifth lecture. Neither Father Lagrange nor Father Batiffol intended to create any turmoil. In 1897, in Fribourg, Father Lagrange had burnt his boats, with pangs of conscience; in 1902, in Toulouse, he expounded, in all serenity, what he thought were assured results. His intention was less to present a manifesto of historical-critical exegesis than an assessment of its results. In Toulouse, Father Lagrange did not express anything that had not already been set out in the *Revue biblique* during the previous ten years. As he explained in his memoirs, the lectures about the historical method, even after they had been published, were not "the explosion of a new system but a simple popularizing of theories that had already been presented, denounced, and examined, without their having been condemned. These theories were now being taught freely even in Rome."

The Toulouse lectures pled for a historical-critical reading of the Bible, even though the new exegesis went against many conventional views defended by "the old conservative party." From the church's viewpoint, with the cultural resources that the present time offered, historical exegesis enriches the Christian community with a better understanding of scripture. As for scholarship, the Catholic exegete's obligation to respect the authority of the church does not set any arbitrary limit to his research, since the believing acceptance of the Bible in the church is part of the very constitution of scripture. To interpret scripture according to the church is to respect the founding relationship that binds the church and scripture together. If it is to respect the nature of its object, the critical reading of the Bible cannot be reduced to a simple chapter in the history of religions.

The historical-critical reading of the Bible does damage a certain type of literal exegesis practiced in the nineteenth century that theologians wrongly swallowed and endowed with an absolute value. Different from the reading practiced in the early church, some "modern" interpretation brought on an impoverishment that Father Lagrange depicted as "isolated, turning ceaselessly in the same circle, taking everything literally by following only the literal sense, forgetting even that the literal sense includes metaphor and allegory, swimming in the absolute, seeing affirmations everywhere, and feeling no astonishment at possessing a real and authentic history of the whole human race from its very beginnings." The Bible reveals the history of salvation. It does not contain the annals of humanity. Whatever, in the Bible, appears as historical is not necessarily history: One must judge it according to the *literary genre* of the narratives. This is particularly true for primitive history (Gen 1–11), the particular character of which distinguishes it as much from myth as from history. The first chapters of the Bible are neither history of the human race nor history of one of its branches. "The primitive history is not, strictly speaking, history," Father Lagrange ended his last lecture on November 11. In spite of the intention proclaimed by Father Lagrange and the precautions taken by Monsignor Batiffol, the *Memoirs* tell us that "there was, however, quite a stir. Some conservatives lodged complaints at the archbishop's office about the novelty of the doctrine. Monsignor German…took it upon himself to calm those who were dissatisfied. I will leave to the reader's malice the task of finding out who they were."

At the time, Father Lagrange, writing to the master general that he would be traveling back to Jerusalem, seemed less aware of the seriousness of the reactions but was more explicit about the personality of his opponents. The two Dominican censors, he explained, put no veto on the publication of the lectures. "Here, the impression was good except for a few Jesuits who were dissatisfied to see that our order was doing good work; and to see that I supported my studies from their own authors. The archbishop attended once and showed me his satisfaction."

Father Lagrange, convinced that his performance was by no means provocative, was going to be in the midst of a turmoil he had neither foreseen nor wanted. On the other hand, Monsignor Batiffol felt at once the explosive aspect of those lectures. As early as November 19, he hastened to warn the master general against the expected outcome:

> It is only our duty to thank you for having been kind enough to allow Father Lagrange to give us, in Toulouse, the six lectures he has delivered. Their success was

greatly due to the current interest in the questions he treated. However, there was some very sharp opposition that, naturally, I came to hear of. This opposition is due, I believe, to the fact that the audience, or some of its members, were not prepared sufficiently to understand all that was said, and that is their fault. It is also due to certain controversial remarks against some exegetes or publicists belonging to the Society of Jesus whom the Reverend Father criticized, very accurately, it is true, but a more irenic exposition would have spared him reproach. Finally, while Father Lagrange's theological doctrine is, we believe, absolutely sound, we think that some applications of this method were of a sort as to sur- prise or trouble even some otherwise favorably disposed minds, not to mention those not favorably disposed. It seems to me, therefore, opportune, both for the safety of your order and for that of our institute, that I should ask your Reverence to have the text of the conference, which will be submitted to you, examined again, carefully, because the examination of them by two of your priests before they were delivered to the audience at the insti- tute overlooked, I think, the minor flaws mentioned, flaws which could cause us all serious unpleasantness, the day these lectures are printed. I rely, Most Reverend Father, upon your prudence to treat this letter as absolutely confidential.

Following the usual way of dealing with Father Lagrange's publications, the master general's approval would be given directly on the page proofs. This method made it easier for the censors to read the text and to make the revisions required. In spite of the criticisms aroused by the lectures, which Rome had requested Toulouse to clarify, the approval seems to have been easily granted. "Reverend Father Paban, censor, having some doubts about the sixth lecture (the primitive history), the

Reverend Father Frühwirth wanted to read it himself and to give the *imprimatur*." The book, 2,000 copies printed, was published in Paris at the beginning of March 1903, bearing the title *Historical Criticism of the Old Testament* (English translation, London, 1906). The purely fortuitous coincidence with the publication of Loisy's *The Gospel and the Church* conferred on Father Lagrange's work an additional timeliness. The book was successful. Copies were sold out in a year, and another 3,000 copies were printed in 1904 under a shorter title, *The Historical Method*. The unchanged text was preceded by a note, "For the Second Printing," in which Father Lagrange forcefully reaffirmed his basic positions.

Father Lagrange claimed for himself the free use of good methods of criticism and of exegesis.

> However confused the situation may be, it is less grievous for Catholicism than the stagnation that existed twenty years ago. The worst is that we Catholics were pleased with ourselves, even ignoring those *irrisiones infidelium* [mockeries of the unbelievers] St. Thomas claims we should avoid. Burying our heads in the sand cannot solve any burning problem. This is where sincerity—the price of a passing scandal—is better than the dissimulation that perpetuates the evil. Because the Bible is a mixed matter, the Catholic exegete must submit his work as much to the critical judgment of the scholarly world as to the dogmatic judgment of the church, for any scholarly inadequacy in his research would do harm to the church. What would then be passed off under the name of Catholic exegesis would hurt our faith as much as reckless innovations, and would tend to create a state of mind unworthy of the intellectual honor of the church. Now, modern exegesis must undergo a severe purification. Alongside the dogmas of faith, the exegetes, not the church, have burdened themselves with many so-called *historical* or

literary dogmas, a heavier and heavier weight that has become quite intolerable in a century introduced to the knowledge of the ancient Near East.

Father Lagrange continued his thought. "This is where we should shed some light and listen to criticism with all due tactfulness. He who speaks of criticism, speaks of caution and circumspection, but it is good to know that we enjoy complete freedom to make good use of all the knowledge acquired in our time." The popes had already shown the way: "Leo XIII, by creating the Biblical Commission, and Pius X, by organizing the doctorate in holy scripture, have obviously wanted the studies to be carried on in a spirit of respect for dogma and attention to solid and conscientious scholarship. All Catholics believe this contribution possible. The future will show it realized."

Father Lagrange's proud, but magnanimous, appraisal was too optimistic. The first reactions to *The Historical Method* might have led one to suspect this. The spectrum ran from the extreme left to the extreme right. First, on Father Loisy's side, Duschesne congratulates him for Father Lagrange's boldness. "The other day they made me read Father Lagrange's lectures in Toulouse, published with the seal of the authorities, and I noted that these oh-so-orthodox people throw overboard a good bit of sacred history. I need not tell you that the author's abominable style and the cowardice he shows when speaking of you have made me sick to my stomach. But it is all the same amusing that one can have come to this point." Father Laberthonnière, too, felt closer to Father Loisy than to Father Lagrange. "I have just finished reading Father Lagrange's book, *The Historical Method*. As a whole I find it weak. The author does not know how to think or to write. He seems to believe that philosophy and theology are matters of common sense. He expects the solution to everything to come from history. And under these conditions, he hardly knows what to look for. Certainly, Loisy is another man." The philosopher, Maurice Blondel, shows more moderation. "Father Lagrange's lectures in

Toulouse have been published with, of course, the imprimatur! And, in brief, there are some truly bold statements in it, wrapped in diplomatic formulae. Many are legitimate, while others are questionable; one can at least regret that they should be necessary." As for one of the most passionate champions of fundamentalism, he assailed Father Lagrange in *La verité française*, accusing him of getting rid of the Pentateuch, "denying and affirming without proofs," as it takes his fancy. "Instead of studying the Germans so carefully, had he not better read over the encyclicals and the decretals and the Council of Trent? And," he maintained against Father Lagrange, "it is a dogma promulgated by Adam or rather by God Himself" that woman was fashioned out of the man's rib.

In Rome, the volume was offered as a courtesy to the cardinals of the Biblical Commission, without anyone, for the time being, finding anything to say against it. From Louvain, Father Lagrange received firm approval from Father Albin van Hoonacker. "The principles you expound and justify so well," van Hoonacker wrote on March 29, 1903, "are those which I myself also consider as the only true ones." Affirmation came from Father Paulin Ladeuze who would later support Father Lagrange when the attacks against him came to a crescendo. However, by publishing *The Historical Method*, Father Lagrange definitively alienated himself from the conservative camp without winning the support of the innovators. They remained implacably hostile to any distancing from the literalness of scripture. The innovators would never forgive Father Lagrange for having stood against Loisy in the name of theology. Father Lagrange was now marked with the regrettable reputation of having ruined the historicity of the Bible, a reputation that would follow him until his death. *The Historical Method* would fuel an endless dispute. Father Lagrange had only tried to adjust the scholarly reading of scripture to the reading practiced by the believing community. He had not accomplished his goal on the first try. He had put together a conception of history, which was too positivist, with a conception of dogma, which was too fundamentalist. He was a man of his time in an age that was still groping for a solution. His main contribution lies in the irreversible orientation he gave to biblical studies.

The Holy See acknowledged the service rendered to the church by the École biblique in Jerusalem. Father Lagrange, who had been nominated consultant to the Biblical Commission on January 21, 1903, was summoned to Rome on February 1. Cardinal Rampolla, president of the commission, asked, in the name of the pope, that the director of the *Revue biblique* come and settle in Rome. Lagrange's mission there would be to publish the review, which was to become the organ of the commission, and to found there an institute of higher biblical studies, supported by the pope. A contract was agreed upon between the two parties and approved by the pope on March 28. "Had Pope Leo XIII lived two months more, the institute would have been created. What had, up until then, held up its realization was that no convenient premises could be found for it." Noted a secretary of the Biblical Commission: "It would have been the ruin of the church [M. Vigouroux said to Father Fonck]."

Two weeks before Easter, which fell on April 12 that year, Father Lagrange asked permission to go back to Jerusalem for a visit. Pope Leo XIII agreed, "Go back to Jerusalem for Easter. Then you will come back. I will have you working near us." Father Lagrange was never to see Leo XIII again. The pope died on July 20. With the election of Pope Pius X, on August 4, the plans elaborated during the former pontificate were placed on a back shelf. A time of trial for historical-critical exegesis ensued.

Chapter VI

TRIALS: THE BANNED BOOKS

The election of Pope Pius X to the See of Peter (August 4, 1903) and the election of Hyacinthe-Marie Cormier as the head of the Dominican Order (May 21, 1904) marked the beginning of a period of suspicion and repression. Father Lagrange would feel the painful consequences of these events.

A surge of intolerance swiftly followed the death of Pope Leo XIII (July 20, 1903). "Times have changed since July 20," admitted Monseigneur Duchesne in a letter to Loisy in November. "The hand which held back the hot coals is no longer here. They will now gather all by themselves. What can be expected from those who claimed the verse about the three witnesses is authentic? They are now upheld by Monseigneur Merry del Val [new secretary of state] who would rather believe that Jonah swallowed the whale than to allow anyone to doubt the contrary."

Father Lagrange's book, *La méthode historique*, found a fierce opponent in the Belgian Jesuit, Alphonse Delattre, who was known as an Orientalist but who, up until then, had not come to public notice in the field of biblical studies. In 1904 in Liège, he published his comments in a book entitled *Autour de la question biblique, une nouvelle école d'exegésè et les autoritiés qu'elle invoque (The Biblical Question, a New School of Exegesis and the Authorities They Invoke)*. Father Lagrange believed that Father Delattre, desiring to keep the church from disastrous doctrine, "thought he would manage this more certainly by discrediting the authority of *La méthode historique* than by refuting the method itself."

Is it legitimate to try to harmonize a historical reading of the Bible with the doctrine of the church as Father Lagrange had sought to do? Father Delattre's book never came to grips with the modern approach as it bore on the inspiration of scripture. Instead, he accused Father Lagrange of having used a totally fallacious argument. According to Father Delattre, neither the fathers of the church, especially Jerome, nor Pope Leo XIII's encyclical letter, *Providentissimus Deus*, permitted or recommended the application of a historical method of interpreting the Bible in which everything was not taken literally. According to Father Delattre, as read by Father Lagrange, "Every attempt to reconcile modern criticism with the ancient principles is fatally doomed to failure." Father Lagrange noted, "If this demonstration chances to rejoice the hearts of a few noteworthy conservatives, is it not bound to discourage many souls of good will?"

Delattre's attack proved to be the first skirmish in a concerted offensive against the historical method. Father Lagrange believed the movement to be directed by Luis Martin, superior general of the Society of Jesus. A letter from this superior dated November 4, 1904, to the provincials of the society, warning them against a process of subversion called "the historical method," had opened the hostilities. On this occasion, Father de Hummelauer, a world-renowned Jesuit exegete, was removed from biblical studies. In Rome, Father Gismondi, who taught biblical exegesis at the Gregorian University, was relegated to the teaching of Near Eastern languages and replaced by Father Delattre, whose book against Father Lagrange had earned him the favor of Pope Pius X.

Was Father Lagrange mistaken in imagining the plot he imputed to the Society of Jesus? Was he arbitrarily attributing to their leader the hostile plan of a few of its members? Whatever the true answer to these question might have been, Father Lagrange's reaction was certain. It revealed a conviction that he often expressed later in life. When he wrote his *Personal Reflections and Memoirs*, in March 1926, he spoke of a directive given from the top and punctiliously obeyed. "It is really under the impetus of the central authorities of the society that so many works were published against the one they called 'the head of the broad school.'" He came back to the subject at the celebration of his jubilee in 1935. In an article paying tribute to Father Lagrange, the Jesuit Joseph Bonsirven recalled that, ever since the fight against Modernism had begun, the vanguard combatant had "felt the weight of high and constant suspicion" on him. As Father Lagrange commented to the master general, "the spirit of the article [Father Bonsirven's article] is certainly that those suspicions were not justified, that they had not touched the heart of the matter, and that the hostile measures were only motivated by the circumstances of the time. What Father Bonsirven, SJ, could not say was that these suspicions were systematically organized by the Company of Jesus, under the direction of Father Martin." [Lagrange's suspicions about Father Luis Martin's campaign against him have now found further documentary support in David G. Schultenover, S.J., *A View From Rome. One the Eve of the Moderinst Crisis* (New York: Fordham University Press, 1993).]

Facing the attack launched against him, Father Lagrange claimed the right of self-defense, not so much to publish his own apology as to claim the thought of Pope Leo XIII. "It is important," he had affirmed, "that the authority of Pope Leo XIII should not be taken away from us." Now, under the reign of Pope Pius X, Father Lagrange was unable to publicly present his defense. Two hundred copies of his *Éclaircissement sur la méthode historique à propos d'un livre du R. P. Delattre, S. J.*, had been published *pro manuscripto* by Lecoffre in 1905, for restricted sale only, and it would remain an almost underground work by the will of his superiors. The conditions of restricted sale publications were that the books not mention the approval of the censors or the permission of the master general. The book had been submitted to them, however, and it had been approved by Father Kaiser, the official censor of Father Lagrange's writings, but its normal commercial distribution had not been authorized by the master general. Only the cardinals and the consultors of the Biblical Commission were sent a copy. The public only heard indirectly about it. Lagrange would have preferred a normal distribution. "This *pro manuscripto*," Father

Lagrange wrote to the superior general, "will astonish people in France, and seem terribly Jesuit-like." His prior in Jerusalem, Father Séjourné, also fought for publicity for *Éclaircissement*: "for the defense of truth and the rightful honor of our school in Jerusalem and of Father Lagrange."

All these efforts were in vain. In Rome, the curia of the order had reproached the *Éclaircissement*, saying it was not doctrinal enough in some areas, nor firm enough in others. He did not recommend any alterations to improve it. "I did not mean to write a treatise," argued Father Lagrange, "but only to show how unfair Father Delattre's attacks are. I think one should grant that I have done that." He apologized for the weakness of his written comments. "I am well aware that this controversy will not cover me with glory; I saw only an opportunity of doing a little good by clarifying the issues." In October 1907, Father Delattre repeated the offense by replying in print to the *Éclaircissement* and thus put Father Lagrange in a cowardly light, presenting him as not having dared a public confrontation.

This new lampoon by Father Delattre cried out for a public response, as Father Lagrange suggested to the master general. "It seems to me that his relentlessness could incline you to permit me to publish a small brochure, and that really nobody could find anything against my using so moderately my right of self-defense. In case this were your opinion, there would be a very simple way of doing it unobtrusively. It would be to publish textually the aforesaid *Éclaircissement* as an appendix to the fifth edition of one thousand copies of *La méthode historique* which is about to be published, as you allowed, and then adding a few notes to repulse the new attacks, very mildly." But the battle against Modernism had rendered the climate less and less favorable to Father Lagrange's open views; the conservative views, which appeared safer, were at a premium. The master general would not allow Father Lagrange to answer Father Delattre publicly, nor to republish *La méthode historique*, unless he agreed to rewrite it or to add major "corrections" that would allow it to coincide with the decrees of the Biblical

Commission. Father Cormier advocated republishing the book but "corrected and improved with the help of the papal documents that have been published since and also in light of the scandals and apostasies that have saddened the church. Some of those men were friends of our Fathers; there was a certain community of ideas, and when they took the fatal step, they reproached us with not having gone to the end of the adopted premises." Father Lagrange could not, without having betrayed his convictions, give up his historic method to join the camp of the conservatives.

At the time, Father Lagrange saw in the discretion imposed on him by Father Cormier the hard trial he would have to suffer: The victim did not benefit from the same liberty as the attacker. Although his honor as a Christian had been challenged, he would not be permitted to defend it. "I answered Father Delattre but was not allowed to publish that answer. He seems to have freedom to attack me, but there is no freedom for me to defend myself. Patience....Nobody comes to my help, as if it were not in the general interest. To go on under such circumstances, one must be fully aware of the urgent needs of souls." Father Lagrange was too fond of free discussion to want to silence his opponents. "I am too sincere a friend of freedom of speech, which is necessary to writers for the dignity of the church, to silence them," he wrote to the master general on another occasion. "But I beg you to give me a little freedom to respond every now and then." To Father Lagrange, the sense of honor was as important as the love of liberty. "Long experience has convinced me that one must never permit one's orthodoxy and one's honesty to become suspect. It is often necessary to reply, to defend one's honor as a Christian and one's honesty."

Although Father Lagrange was not permitted to answer him, Father Delattre did not win in the long run. He did enjoy a transient victory in 1920, however, with the publishing of the encyclical *Spiritus Paraclitus*, in which the literal authenticity of the events experienced by Lot's wife is asserted. In the end, Father Cormier probably did Father Lagrange a service by preventing him from taking up the struggle on the grounds chosen by Father

Delattre. A brief and vigorous article going to the heart of the matter would have been worth more than endless quibbles about passages from St. Jerome or Pope Leo XIII's encyclical. Under the circumstances, it, too, would probably have been doomed to oblivion like many other texts by Father Lagrange.

Whatever its success or failure may have been, *La méthode historique* was not Father Lagrange's major work. It was on Genesis, its attribution to Moses, its composition by different sources, its historical value as the narration of the origins, and the saga of the Patriarchs that he wanted to take a stand. On these points, the Roman authorities never permitted him to explain himself.

At the beginning of 1898, Father Lagrange thought he would be able to launch the series of *Études bibliques* with a commentary on Genesis. "As soon as the commentary on Genesis is published," he wrote to the master general, around the middle of February, "I shall distribute the other volumes of the Bible." As the work was almost finished at the beginning of May, Father Lagrange asked Rome to name two censors to examine the manuscript. The answer came on May 17. "The Most Reverend Father asks him to send his work on Genesis so as to have it examined, as he wishes, by competent judges, before giving it to the printers." The introduction and the commentary on the first three biblical chapters were sent to the master general on June 13. "The rest is almost finished, but it is useless to send it if the main lines of the work are not approved," commented Father Lagrange.

The two censors to whom the manuscript was submitted— Thomas Esser, professor at St. Thomas College in Rome, and Dalmace Sertillanges, professor at the Institut catholique in Paris—agreed that no basic objection could be made against the publication of the commentary. They judged it to be just as irreproachable theologically as it was academically. "The book, even if it surprises by the critical positions it upholds, shows its respect for the Word of God and does not deviate from the teaching of the church." The censors diverged as to the timeliness of publishing the work, however. Father Sertillanges felt that they must have the courage to clear the air surrounding biblical discussion and not hesitate to do the work of truth. Father Esser, on the other hand, thought theologians were too ignorant of the latest historical advancements to accept a critical explanation of Genesis without strongly resisting it. Rather than provoke them by publishing the book, he felt it would be better to familiarize them through articles on limited points; otherwise, the book might be condemned, and that would hurt the cause it was meant to serve. His advice having prevailed, Father Lagrange yielded to it without balking and produced for the October issue of the *Revue biblique* an essay on Genesis, chapter 49, "Jacob's Prophecy." He presented the method followed in the larger commentary and hoped to solicit the advice of competent readers.

The result was the reverse of what he'd hoped for. To begin with, Prior Le Vigoureux, at St. Stephen priory itself, was by no means won over. "You must know that Father Lagrange sticks to his ideas and to his method, in spite of the observations that were addressed to him from Rome. The latest issue of the *Revue biblique* contains an article by him on Jacob's prophecy, which I find rash. It must, moreover, be part of his commentary on Genesis, the publication of which it seems wiser to postpone, at the least." He warned his correspondent, the provincial of the Dominicans in Paris, against any laxity in the control of the *Revue biblique*, especially if Father Séjourné were to be its secretary. "It is quite clear that Father Séjourné will let anything pass. That is what Father Lagrange wants." The prior, more devoted to the buildings of St. Stephen priory than to the studies at the École biblique, which in his eyes only led to trouble, was the person whom Father Lagrange no longer dared to ask for the sums necessary to buy books, even those he needed most.

In September, Father Lagrange asked for the master general's advice: "If you think that a year will suffice to arrive at an opportune moment, we can start the printing, for we will need that time to set it up, especially with my being in Jerusalem." The master general answered at the end of October: "[He must] wait before publishing his work." Neither of the two masters, Father Frühwirth or Father Cormier, would ever alter his decision, even after further consultations with experts. Father Lagrange received this decision, which hurt him, with his customary obedience. "I remain quite submitted to your decision as to *my* Genesis, but I cannot hide from you how unhappy I feel when I see what we produce among Catholics." About an approved book, which he accused of being "a dishonor to Catholic science," Father Lagrange commented further: "It is allowed to pass because it pretends to uphold the Catholic cause in an intransigent way, while one considers as dangerous a much surer but moderate defense that takes facts into account! Well, let us wait, if we have to!" A few weeks later, Father Lagrange stated his position once again in regard to the orders he had received from the master general of the order. "I am rather surprised that you should think me capable of having *my* Genesis printed without your leave. Thank God, such a thought is far from me. I cruelly feel our inferiority as to critical studies, but I quite well know that nothing can be remedied in the church outside [the framework] of obedience."

When an article on the Flood, written for the *Revue biblique*, found no more favor in the eyes of the Roman censors than the commentary on Genesis, Father Lagrange bowed without recrimination. "You do not insist," wrote the master general, "and I congratulate you on that, for the difficulties are even greater than you imagine. The main thing is that your work would certainly have been put on the Index; your future would have been jeopardized, and the stain would have blemished our order. Under such conditions, we could not approve your work."

"If only we could have the chance to explain our views on that [biblical] history," lamented Father Lagrange. As he declared in the *Revue biblique* in January 1906, he would like to have explained how the history of origins [Genesis, chapters 1 to 11] differs as much from the religious myths of the ancient Near East as from the pseudohistorical novels of Greek literature. The story of the Patriarchs [Genesis, chapters 12 to 50] offered him a field of observation in which primitive history and popular legends were closely linked. To offer an instance of his method of interpretation, he had prepared, in January 1905, an article entitled *The Patriarchs: How They Belong to History*, which the censors deemed unpublishable. One censor judged it untimely, the other found it intolerable. According to the latter, "Lagrange's hypotheses are nothing but the dreams of the German and English rationalists that he has translated into French. He has been reading those critics too much and lets himself be guided by them. His articles, especially the latest on the Patriarchs, are extremely dangerous (like Loisy's books on the New Testament). For the honor of our order, to avoid scandals, for the sake of Lagrange himself, he must not be allowed to publish these articles." Lagrange, who would have liked to publish the article in the *Revue biblique* of January 1906, thought that such a limited study would favor a gentle and prudent progress of historical-critical exegesis. The master general, given the advice of the censors, first ordered him to postpone the publication, then to give it up altogether. The positions held by Lagrange left Cormier reticent. "I have read the article several times. I have discussed it with Lagrange and have not yet quite understood what, in these composite characters, can be really assigned to the Patriarchs in flesh and blood and what belongs to the ideas, tales, and legendary trends then current, which may have been blended with these characters. Neither can one see clearly enough why one should resort to this conception." By 1906, critical audacity was no longer in vogue. "The Patriarchs" became a dead issue.

Lagrange questioned the decision. "Does not using coercion harm the intellectual vitality of the church? Would it not be better to allow the expression of moderate, even if somewhat new, opinions?" Lagrange, even though still convinced that the silence imposed upon the moderates boosted the extremists, yielded without protest to the orders of his superior. Each person is given his own responsibility. One has to order, the other has to obey. Obedience was to demand even crueler sacrifices. The first would involve his commentary on Genesis.

"If we are given the opportunity to publish our commentary on Genesis," declared Father Lagrange in his *Éclaircissement*," the reader will be able to judge how far we are from myth and how religious tradition is rather illumined than compromised by the movement of critical studies." The publication of the commentary on Genesis, which was to open the series *Études bibliques*, had been postponed, awaiting more favorable circumstances. Lagrange was not prepared to allow the stifling of his work. At intervals, he would ask the master general, "What about *my* Genesis? It is most important to me." At the end of 1904, he returned to the matter once again with Cormier, presenting his manuscript for a new examination. Then, a few months later, the master general seemed ready to let the book be printed, if not to put the whole volume immediately into the hands of the public, at least to submit some of its chapters to the Biblical Commission. "Let me thank you warmly," responded Lagrange on March 17, 1905. "Please be assured that I shall be as tractable, as full of goodwill as possible, to facilitate the task of the examiners. I am sure Father Kaiser will be rather pleased and so will the public. It seems my *Éclaircisse-ment*…is considered insufficiently doctrinal, not decisive enough.…The commentary on Genesis will offer the best possible clarification.…The approval you have given to the printing of Genesis proves that I was wrong in thinking you mistrusted me, and I beg you to forgive me for having so stridently said so."

Father Sertillanges, consulted again, declared that although the work did go against many widely accepted opinions held by most Catholics, it was theologically irreproachable: "…scientific truth is not a matter of majority opinion." As to timeliness, the censor considered that it was essential for Catholic scholars to be given the widest possible latitude, since the limits of Catholic scholarship were indefinite. "Indeed, in the present state of scholarship, this freedom is the only way for Catholic exegetes to find respect among their opponents, instead of being classified among those who are ruled by groundless prejudice, if not among weak-minded children. Such classification is to the great detriment of our religion and of our souls." Although he recognized the apostolic necessity of critical work to strengthen the faith of those who yield to the seductions of novelty, Father Lagrange knew that the cause he was fighting for had not yet been won. He remained peacefully submissive to the will of his superior. On July 23, 1905, he wrote:

> I will not add anything regarding *my* Genesis. Indeed, I have resolved…not to ask God anything but that his Holy Will be done as to this question. I cannot, however, help seeing the evil you point out among young priests and seminarians. This evil, which is probably much deeper than you think, will lead to revolts, at least secret ones, will lose many a priestly soul, and will only cease, except for some extraordinary God-given grace, when minds have found their peace again. Their peace lies in the recognition that the church will tolerate serious and honest exegesis. Such exegesis will certainly have its defects and errors of detail but will respect dogma by showing sufficiently its concern for truth.

At the end of October 1905, after several months of consideration, Father Cornier still preferred to defer any publication on this burning subject. "I think it is wiser, unless I am given better lights from within or from without, not to publish, just now, anything on Genesis, be it an article, such as the one [on the Patriarchs] whose publication we have suspended, or a book. This deferring will benefit whatever may be published later on, either through its intrinsic merit or through its moral authority." The master general had been waiting for the decision of the Biblical Commission to guide his decision. Whichever way Father Lagrange turned, he always got the same dilatory answer. The answer given by Pope Pius X himself to Father Séjourné's request in January 1906 provides an example. Father Séjourné wrote, "Holy Father, Father Lagrange has been prepared for a long time with a commentary on Genesis and would like to publish it." The pope's answer was almost immediate: "It is difficult just now. [You] had better wait for the decisions and documents that are being prepared." When the Biblical Commission made its pronouncement, by decree on June 27, 1906, on the Mosaic authenticity of the Pentateuch (which it, of course, imposed, except for a few nuances), Cormier wrote to Lagrange, and concluded: "As to your work on Genesis, I very much doubt that it corresponds exactly to the views and spirit of the latest decree of the commission....It is true that the fourth paragraph touching the interpolations after Moses' death does moderate them by repeating some things that have already been admitted, so that the Holy See may not be accused of intransigence and solidarity with certain conservative groups. But, unless I am mistaken, this is still far from some theories or hypotheses [you maintain], and the totality of the decree is rather a warning than an opening."

Finally, the verdict was received. It was relayed in a notification from the Secretary of State to the master general, dated May 27, 1907. On behalf of the Holy Father, Cardinal Merry del Val demanded that Father Cormier forbid any publication of the commentary on Genesis, even in the form of page proofs reserved for the use of an initiated few. The work, as he saw it, was inspired by criteria opposed to those upheld by the Biblical Commission. On the same day, the introduction to the Book of Isaiah, prepared by Father Condamin, SJ, for the series *Études bibliques*, was similarly prohibited. As soon as Father Lagrange learned about the measure, he expressed his submission to the pope.

On June 9, he made his submission official:

Most Holy Father, postrate at the feet of Your Holiness, I accept, with the most filial obedience, your decision, communicated to me through the master general of our order, forbidding me to publish, in any way whatsoever, a commentary on Genesis. But it is not enough to obey Your Holiness' orders. I have therefore resolved to consider even your wishes as orders. If, then, Your Holiness deems it preferable that

I cease working on biblical studies, I will give them up immediately without any hesitation. I am not the type to submit and then continue. I only beseech Your Holiness to deign to believe in the right intention that has inspired me up to now. The measure Your Holiness has taken in my regard makes me fear I have been mistaken, and it would now be impossible for me to write the slightest line with the awareness that I am disobeying the instructions of Your Holiness.

Father Cormier, by demanding that Father Lagrange give up work on the Old Testament altogether, had gone beyond the Holy Father's orders. Father Lagrange did not haggle over this point.

I need not tell you that I accept His Holiness' decision with the greatest deference. I must tell you, however, that I would have preferred that this matter not have been referred to the Holy Father in person; that goes far beyond the canonical rules, already so strict about the printing of books! But now that it has been submitted to him, I wish he would settle the matter. For a long time, I have been telling you of the pangs of my conscience at writing on biblical questions in a way that had, it seems, the full approve of Pope Leo XIII. I am, therefore, writing so that he may deign to settle me, and I would be grateful if you would be willing to transmit my letter to him. Up until now, I did not want to trouble him about myself, but since it has begun, what I fear is that he might ask me to write but in a strictly conservative sense. That I cannot do. According to my conscience that would be to betray the church and the truth....To keep silent and to stop working on the Bible, that I would willingly do, as I have often told you.

The Holy Father had asked Father Lagrange neither for "a recantation that nobody would take seriously and that would do more harm than good," nor for a withdrawal into silence by giving up biblical exegesis. Far from being discouraged, Father Lagrange switched to work on the New Testament, undertaking a commentary on the Gospel of Mark. The failure of the commentary on Genesis, imposed by Pope Pius X, in person, would not break Father Lagrange's career as an exegete after all.

Chapter VII

THE REPRIMAND FROM ROME

Beginning in 1907, the struggle by the church authorities against those labeled *Modernists* intensified. Modernists were suspected of sacrificing the Christian faith to modern culture under the pretext of harmonizing the two. The Holy Office became an organ of repression by excommunicating the Modernists; the Index, by prohibiting their written work; the Biblical Commission, by stifling exegetical research; and the Consistorial Congregation, by controlling the teaching in seminaries. The worst was that the Roman Congregations were often roused to action by anonymous informers. Those denounced were powerless to defend themselves against their accusers. Under the leadership of Monsignor Benigni, these anonymous informers were later organized into a clandestine network.

Among the repressive measures, some were merely a matter for ordinary administration. Such was the case of the apostolic visitations entrusted to zealous inquisitors charged by Rome with the job of inspecting the dioceses. Cardinal Ferrari, the archbishop of Milan, who had suffered such visitations, called them "apostolic vexations." Similarly, the purge of scripture professors in Italian seminaries occurred after the inquisitors had inspected the students' class notes. Other, more solemn measures belonged to the magisterial level in the sense that they involved the teaching authority of the church. These measures are outlined in the decree *Lamentabili* (July 3, 1907), the encyclical *Pascendi* (September 8, 1907), and the *motu proprio Sacrorum antistitum* (September 1, 1910) which imposed the anti-Modernist oath on the clergy. To judge from the reflection the Bollandist Hippolyte

Delehaye offered to Father Lagrange, 1907 must have appeared to have been a terrible year. As to Delattre's attack against *La méthode historique*, Delehaye considered it despicable, but he knew also that the pope himself had approved it. "Alas!" Father Delehaye exclaimed. "It seems…that in high places, everything is judged *good* against the specter of Modernism. Let us hope that salvation will come from the very excess of the reaction. What a blow to the prestige of the Holy See!"

What were Father Lagrange's sentiments about the acts of Rome against Modernism? The decree *Lamentabili* proposed sixty-five proscriptions on what were considered errors of principle. These proposals did not surprise Father Lagrange. For fifteen months, the rumor had spread that the Holy See was preparing a new syllabus like the one that had distinguished the reign of Pope Pius IX, in 1864. Others discredited this idea. Now, in May 1906, Father Lagrange was becoming anxious. He wrote to his close friends. To Father Henry Hyvernat, on May 21, he wrote, "If you go to Rome, for the love of God, for the honor of the holy church, speak some good words so that one may keep one's head and not lose one's temper because of intransigent Jesuits!" And to Father Albert Condamin on May 27, he wrote:

> We are at the climax of a reaction that will not permit any publication that is the least bit critical.…It is certain that we shall have something from the Holy See before July, but I imagine it will only be against [the work of] Loisy. His supporters are clamoring in various ways for a determination on the propositions, and that is in itself a huge project. They are trying very actively to include me in his condemnation. I feel so innocent that I cannot at all believe that I will be affected by it. In case I am, I have already told you, it will be quickly done: a plain submission and absolute silence. Moreover, I admit that I very well understand this trepidation. There is quite enough to make one shudder

and tremble at seeing the state of so many minds....But where is the remedy?

In October 1907, the *Revue biblique* not only published the text of *Lamentabili*, it also added a well-thought-out comment: "The Decree *Lamentabili Sane Exitu* and Historical Criticism." Father Lagrange expressed his entire satisfaction at the way a difficult problem had been solved: "The rejection of errors has been put forth in the name of criticism and history, without doing the least harm to the reasonable freedom of historical criticism." Even if the decree itself could not bring peace after anxiety, or security after threat, it threw light on the relationship between history and dogma without scoffing at the rights of criticism. "We want to show that the Holy Office did not prevent us from a critical and historical defense of truth, the only way, nowadays, of reaching certain minds." Was this an obligatory apology? Nothing obliged Father Lagrange to publish twelve pages of approval. The letters he wrote during the summer of 1907 leave no doubt as to his good faith. "You see," he wrote to Father Condamin, "that the so-called *syllabus* one dreaded so much is nothing but the detailed condemnation of Loisy. There is not one proposition that can be said to come from the *Revue biblique*, or from any of the publications connected with it, and we have fought against a great number of them. This syllabus should open the eyes of many people." In the same sense, he declared to Father Salvatore Minocchi: "I am very satisfied with the decree *Lamentabili*. The Holy Office has taken a theological view of things and said nothing that shackles Catholic critical studies. There are at least fifty propositions out of sixty-five that are more or less directly aimed at the theories of Loisy."

On the other hand, the encyclical *Pascendi* was neither published nor commented on by the *Revue biblique*, but, recognized the master general, "It has made Father Lagrange happy since it is what he has always taught." Lack of publication or comment did not show reservation. "As it is totally—or almost totally—devoted to philosophy...and to the false methods suggested by a false philosophy, it seems to me that...we may keep silent. Our submission as religious and as Catholics is sufficiently well known. That [silence] would be the solution I would prefer." Father Cormier advocated a public adherence, the text of which, prepared by Father Lagrange, satisfied neither of them. Father Lagrange could not make too much of the subject without being suspected of fawning, nor make too little, without being accused of spite. Consequently, they never published the submission of the Biblical School in the *Revue biblique*. Except for Father Delattre, nobody could believe the Father Lagrange was the target of the encyclical. Father Lagrange wrote to Father Xavier Faucher on November 24, 1907, "I was glad to see that not one review, even among the most hostile, referred to us as being among those denounced by the pontifical documents. I think we owe this to our faithfulness to St. Thomas. Theologically, there has never been anything to say against us, and it is obviously from that side [theological] that the danger comes which they condemn." To Albert Condamin, on December 6, he wrote, "I only see that Father Delattre has cunningly tried to associate me with Modernism. Let him go on with his solitary fencing. I really think it is of no great consequence."

On September 1, 1910, when the *motu propio Sacrorum antistitum* ordered them to take the oath against Modernism, the professors of the Biblical School, beginning with Father Lagrange, signed the formula without the slightest hesitation. Father Lagrange signed because he could see that, on the whole, the measures taken by Rome against Modernism were an indispensable clarification that he deemed necessary to remedy the extreme confusion of minds. The extremist positions denounced by the pontifical documents were those that the *Revue biblique* had been fighting against from the beginning. If he resolutely gave his adherence to the anti-Modernist oath, it was because this oath did not seem to him incompatible with his own position, while he absolutely refused to side, out of opportunism, with the conservative positions of Father Fulcran Vigouroux. In that case, it was better to say nothing than to make concessions. This silence had nothing to do with the respectful silence of the Jansenists.

The Holy See had condemned Modernism according to a procedure "that has seemed opportune...to him who alone is judge of what is opportune." Although Father Lagrange adhered to the condemnation, he realized that the efficacy of such repressive measures was doubtful. "We must not forget that Loisy's attempt was, among others, a very sincere effort of refutation and apology. Though it failed, the difficulties remain unresolved difficulties, we must say, that are unknown to many who think they have triumphed easily and noisily over them." During the summer of 1909, Father Lagrange felt alarmed by the triumphs of the reactionaries. "Where are we going?" he wrote to Father Hyvernat.

> God knows! Reaction is in full swing while revolt is brewing, cause and effect being mutual. Little by little, a system of so-called *progress of dogma* is building up, which, in fact, only distorts it. Father Loisy's doctrine is smoldering under the embers and spreading quietly by appealing to the church of tomorrow. In Rome, they think the remedy to this situation is Father Delattre's bloc. If you have a bit of zeal for the *good* of the church, try to make some people understand that the bloc no longer holds and that fire can only be fought by fire. Here, we would like to uphold the whole dogmatic structure by a little liberty in historical criticism. In Rome, they think they are very strong because no one resists them openly, but they do not know how many are losing interest and heart. And for us who want to work for the good, they dither over giving us an imprimatur about which the others could not care less.

Both before and after the anti-Modernist campaign, Father Lagrange kept repeating that "only criticism can cure criticism."

Ever since his research on the Pentateuch had been interrupted in 1907, Father Lagrange had stopped work on his study of the Old Testament, without however giving up the study of the Bible altogether. In 1908, he set to work on the Gospel of Mark. He was preparing a learned commentary, "directed," he said, "against liberal exegesis and Father Loisy." He talked about his intentions on several occasions in 1909. On March 19, he wrote, "In my mind, the commentary is designed to refute Loisy's heterodox theories and to replace them, for one only refutes well what one can replace." On April 18, he wrote, "I believe it my duty to waste no time and to try to counterbalance Loisy's bad influence.... The best way to counter his influence would be to do a commentary on the Gospel that would be at once a refutation and a more solid work." At the same time, Father Lagrange was wondering whether the projected work could manage the hurdle of Roman censorship. In fact, his *St. Mark* was only published after several years of bitter negotiations, such as those that had preceded the rejection of his Genesis.

In March 1909, Father Lagrange had sent the first six chapters to the master general as a sample of his work. "Of course, if this attempt is approved, the rest will be sent in due course. I ask you, and the examiners you will be kind enough to appoint, to have the charity to let me know [your decision], so I won't heap manuscripts on top of manuscripts and end up with a disappointment when I could be spending my time in a more profitable manner. Personally, I really believe there will be no difficulty, for no one has ever reproached me for anything pertaining to the New Testament, but I would like to have some assurance that this kind of commentary will be judged useful." Five months later, Father Lagrange received a chilling warning from Father Cormier. "I recommend that you be cautious and be more reserved in quoting unbelieving authors." Remarks recorded during the interrupted revision of the commentary on Mark were unfavorable: "It is hard to tell whether the author is a priest and a disciple of the church. He so readily quotes unsafe contemporary authorities yet is parsimonious when it comes

to quoting traditional authorities, whose value is greater, even sci-
entifically speaking."

Immediately, and not without testiness, Father Lagrange
asked to withdraw his work. "Since the reviser of *St. Mark* was not
able to see that the author is a priest and a disciple of the church,
nor, even more, that the work is directed against independent modern exegesis and particularly against the work of Loisy, I would be
grateful if you would send the manuscript back to Jerusalem," he
wrote on August 6. Father Lagrange came back to the same subject
on August 25. "I have worked with all my might on a commentary
on St. Mark that is the constant refutation of the rationalist com-
mentators, particularly of Loisy. In this work, I have put all my
heart, everything I know, and all my desire to serve the church, and
all you can say is that one doesn't know if the author is a priest and
a Catholic! Frankly, I am exasperated!" He complained mightily.
"Endless reproofs come from Rome, instead of the encouragement
the professors of the Biblical School are expecting to get." Father
Lagrange was ready to give up publishing his commentary on
Mark, but the master general, alerted by Jerusalem, relaunched
him. "It is true that one of the examiners told me himself that he
thought the book would gain in value, if, in the way it expressed
things, one could feel more clearly the minister of God, the child of
the church. None of its strength against heretics or naturalists
would lose anything by it. But this is far from judging that the publishing of the book cannot be useful." On the very concept of service to the church, a conflict existed. The feeling of the servants of
the ecclesiastical apparatus, locked up in the Catholic world, did not
coincide with the feeling of the exegete, engaged in dialogue with
the scholars of the learned world. Yet, Father Lagrange, standing at
the intersection of two distinct circles, never hesitated to take seriously the modifications imposed by the Roman censors.

Once he had finished the commentary and sent the manuscript to Rome (April 13, 1910), Father Lagrange began, in May,
to write the introduction, a major piece of work in itself. He completed the work and sent it off on July 15. "I find great comfort,"

he wrote on August 8, "when I think that my life is not spent on useless tasks, and that this new book will make people love and know Our Lord in his Gospel. That is, I think, what will emerge from the whole, although it appears purely critical." The book, published in Paris on March 3, 1911, arrived in Jerusalem on March 16. The congratulations sent to Father Lagrange by Cardinal Rampolla, March 18, though they attest that one of the first copies was sent to the president of the Biblical Commission, had come too soon to be based on a serious reading of the work.

Now, by the mere fact of asking critical questions as to the traditional dating of the gospels, their editorial processes, their historical value, Father Lagrange was going to arouse the same suspicions Genesis and *La méthode historique* had. When the gospels, reporting the sayings and the deeds of Jesus, are understood as though they were a congressional report of his every word published in the *Bulletin of the French Republic*, no critical question is admissible. For some, to discuss the positions of Loisy seriously instead of rejecting them out of hand amounted to siding with them, and thus, to moving away from ecclesiastical orthodoxy. In 1912, while the Biblical Commission was preparing a reply on the Gospel of Mark and another one on the synoptic question, an attack against Lagrange's manuscript came from an Italian Jesuit, Father Ilario Rinieri. His articles appeared in an intransigent Milanese journal, *La scuola cattolica e la scienza italiana* (in the issues of March and May 1912). After seeing Father Rinieri's first article, Father Lagrange decided he had to defend himself in an answer addressed to the journal. Father Cormier intervened and would not allow Father Lagrange to publish his response. In his unpublished answer, Father Lagrange, accused of hypercriticism as to the date of the Gospel of Mark, claimed his right to use the legitimate freedom Catholic exegesis enjoys, the same freedom used by so traditional a commentator as Father Fillion, the Sulpician. Moreover, Father Lagrange considered it slanderous to accuse him of supporting his thesis by an imposture, of dishonestly truncating the quotations he cited to uphold his position.

The file opened by the Holy See in 1898 against Lagrange, after his article on the sources of the Pentateuch (Lagrange thought the case had been dropped), started to fill up with new accusations after each disputable publication. Indeed, after the public blame cast upon Lagrange's work on June 29, 1912, and published on August 16, 1912, his work on the Gospel of Mark risked being referred to the Index. On August 13, Lagrange explained to Father Cormier:

> It seems to me that now, especially, I should do something to defend *my St. Mark* against Rinieri's attacks that are being itemized at the Index. I have written some very short observations in the style of the bulletin section of the *Revue biblique*. I've asked Mr. Gabalda to send you a hundred copies. You will see if it would not be appropriate to publish those notes in the *Revue biblique*, to ask that they should immediately be inserted in the *Scuola cattolica* and to communicate them confidentially as information to some influential people at the Holy Office or at the Index. This is not a solemn memorandum to those congregations but a simple note that could dispel many a prejudice with people of good faith. Nothing can be done with the fanatics.

The note from Jerusalem, dated October 13, 1912, published in the October issue of the *Revue biblique*, showed that Father Lagrange's Mark did not contradict the reply published by the Biblical Commission on June 26, 1912, regarding either the priority of Mark, or the Greek text of Matthew, or the authenticity of the longer ending of the Gospel of Mark. The defense set forth by Father Lagrange did not help. His Mark book stood in the list of reasons published on June 29 by the Consistorial Congregation to justify disapproval. According to the congregation, the commentary suffered from the same principles as those used by the *Revue biblique* regarding the sources and the historical value of the biblical writings. It erred in asserting that the Gospel of Mark is one of two sources drawn on by the gospels of Matthew and Luke, thereby pushing back the dates of their composition. Since it attributed to the evangelist "the independence of an author," instead of considering him a simple reporter, it compromised the historical value of the gospel story. None of Lagrange's works, not even his Mark, escaped Roman reprobation.

Professions of faith were demanded. In 1910, Lagrange took the anti-Modernist oath. In 1911, he made a personal declaration of obedience to the Holy See. Nevertheless, an unyielding suspicion continued to weigh on Lagrange, kept alive, no doubt, by the adversaries of the Biblical School of Jerusalem. Accusations would blare brutally from a direction he had least suspected. Among the church institutions then charged with the control of orthodoxy, the Consistorial, after Pope Pius X's reform of the curia in 1908, held as important a place as the Holy Office or the Index. The congregation, whose duty it was to choose the bishops, was also to supervise their government, to assign apostolic visitations, and to receive reports on Modernism in their dioceses. They were charged with controlling the seminaries for their teaching equally as much as for their discipline. Since October 1908, the Consistorial had been run by Cardinal Gaetano de Laï, the strongman of the pontificate, and the protector of the network of denunciation organized by Monsignor Benigni, who was unfavorably disposed toward the Biblical School of Jerusalem and its director. "He [Cardinal Gaetano de Laï] is one of ours," noted Monsignor Benigni in August 1913.

By March 1912, Cardinal Mercier had found it very difficult to get Cardinal de Laï's authorization for the Week of Religious Ethnology planned in Louvain. The chief of the Consistorial had approved, but only on the condition that it would not be used as a platform where Father Lagrange and Father Zapletal (professor of exegesis at Fribourg) could spread their "pernicious and erroneous doctrine." Because Father Lagrange did not plan to take part in that Week, with which his name had been associated in spite of himself, the exclusion imposed by Cardinal de Laï did not trouble him nor alarm the master general. Yet, the rumor was spreading that Father Lagrange's Mark had been denounced to the Index, and that a threat hung over the Biblical School itself. This unverifiable rumor later proved well founded.

Did Father Lagrange receive some premonition of the coming storm? He had been the director of the Biblical School at Jerusalem from its beginning until 1907. He was reelected to the director position once more in 1910. Tired of having too many administrative responsibilities to the detriment of his scientific studies, he had asked Father Cormier to accept his resignation as prior. When the master general accepted his resignation on July 26, 1912, Father Lagrange was no longer the head of St. Stephen priory. Even before his voluntary withdrawal, on Saturday, June 29, he had had a spiritual experience of divine purification. He wrote of it in his *Personal Reflections and Memoirs*. "On that day, June 29, we were celebrating the priestly jubilee of the Franciscan Darlé at Aïn Karim. I had been filled all day long with a very gentle feeling of God's presence. The following night, after a short sleep, I woke with a start. A sudden vision of death filled my mind, as new as if I had only thought of it for the first time. As I was overcome by anguish and could not think of sleeping, I spent the rest of the night in prayer, walking up and down in my cell, incapable of calming that strange terror. Perhaps God wanted me to be ready to set value only on invisible things and on his judgment."

Five weeks later, a decree from the Consistorial arrived in Jerusalem. It had been promulgated precisely on June 29. "On the evening of August 5," recalled Father Vincent, "Father Lagrange gathered his young collaborators, read them the decree, and told them what he would do." The decree of the Consistorial struck a hard blow at historical interpretation. It forbade seminaries to offer the *Special Introduction to the Old Testament*, published in Paderborn by Dr. Karl Holzhey, even as a reference book. The book had been accused of opposing the teaching of the church and of ruining the historical value of the books of the Bible because it had adopted the modern theories of rationalism and hypercriticism. After the first blow, the decree delivered a second. "As there are other identically inspired commentaries on the holy scripture of the Old and New Testaments, such as several works by Father Lagrange and a recent book by Dr. Fritz Tillman on the New Testament, His Holiness orders and proscribes that they, too, be absolutely removed from the curricula of clerics, except where a fuller judgment might be rendered by the appropriate authority." The decree of the Consistorial was reprobation rather than a condemnation. It had been drafted in haste as a temporary measure of protection to check an immediate danger, while awaiting another instance that might be construed dangerous enough to pronounce sentence. The burden of its weight fell directly on Dr. Holzhey. His incriminating book was prohibited by the Index on January 20, 1913. Monsigneur Duchesne had suffered a similar sentence. His *History of the Early Church*, first prohibited by the Consistorial on September 1, 1911, had been placed on the Index on January 22, 1912. A similar sentence was threatening several works of Father Lagrange, starting with his most recent work, *St. Mark*.

Almost immediately, Father Lagrange set out behavioral guidelines for his disciples: "Submit totally, without reservation and on every point." This advice was the same that Father Cormier had given him when he told him he was sending the text of his manuscript for review. On July 27, he wrote, "It is not for me to discuss, judge, or interpret the act of the Holy See. Our duty, and first of all *my* duty, is to bow mentally and wholeheartedly, and to inspire the same feelings in those over whom we have some authority or influence." Father Lagrange suggested even more self-effacement than was required: He offered to leave Jerusalem for one year and to turn the *Revue biblique* into a *Revue des études palestiniennes et orientales*. The intensity of his distress, as well as the promptness of his obedience, can be read in a remembrance of

Father Buzy, who was a biblical teacher and a friend of Father Lagrange.

> In 1912, he arrived one morning in Bethlehem: "Father Buzy, I am finished, condemned!" He handed me the decree of the Consistorial. He cried. "After having worked so much, shown such goodwill, to be struck down by the church!" He told me about the plots woven against him of which he had become the victim. He spoke about it with no bitterness, almost as a historian. "What are you going to do, Father?" I asked. He sat up straight, and with an inimitable accent of faith and simplicity, he said: "What am I going to do? Well, submit!...Moreover, I am leaving Jerusalem immediately, since I have become a danger to the Biblical School. We have also asked the Holy Father if he would like the *Revue biblique* to cease publication."

On August 6, on his way to Rome, Father Lagrange answered Father Cormier, who hastened to have the letter read to Pope Pius X.

> My Reverend Father,
>
> Last night I received the kind letter you sent me July 27, and I am very thankful for the fatherly feelings you show me. I have not yet received the decree from the Consistorial. I think you never doubted my complete submission. Please be kind enough to guide me and show me what I must do in this matter, so that everything may be done properly.
>
> You also ask me to speak to you about St. Stephen's. This, of course, needs some thought. As for me personally, it is clear I must no longer work on holy scripture. To submit and then to start all over again in the same vein would be to imitate Loisy. To choose

another path? Which one? Nobody would take me seriously.

So, I propose to give up the course on holy scripture next year; to discontinue the commentary on Luke; and to write nothing at all on this subject, not even book reviews. This is not because I feel discouraged, but to show myself submissive to the guidance given me by the Holy See, this time very clearly. Therefore, I can no longer continue to edit the *Revue biblique*.

Nobody here, I think, would consent to take it [editing] up. I believe the only practical thing is what I have suggested in a memorandum I sent you, written in Rome in 1905, and that is to change it into a *Revue des études palestiniennes et orientales*. This transformation can only be seen as an act of deference towards the Holy See. I am going to write about it to Mr. Gabalda. If you approve of this project, I shall discuss it with him and we can continue.

Far from arousing the others against authority, I ask them to continue; but, it seems to me, the general opinion is that we have every reason to limit ourselves to Oriental and archaeological questions, outside of the Bible, except for topography, as Cardinal Rampolla often advised me to do.

Had we only followed that path in 1905, as I often asked you to let us do!

Besides, our father subprior is coming home on Friday or Monday. We will hold our elections, and we will tell you what the general opinion is here.

As for my own self, didn't I often tell you that I should count for nothing? Even if you consider that it is more convenient to send me elsewhere, so much the better. At the very least, I would not be sorry to have a year's leave.

The school itself could very well be considered a school of Palestinian and Oriental studies. It seems to me, you could quite easily present this step as an act deferential to the intentions of the Holy Father. Here we are ready for it.

As for recriminations by letters, I dare say it is not in my character.

Please, my Reverend Father, give me your blessing and your prayers, and believe in my deep respect.

Pope Pius X, before whose eyes Father Cormier immediately placed Father Lagrange's letter, could only rejoice. "I read Father Lagrange's beautiful letter with the utmost care, and you will have the kindness to answer him that I was quite assured of his feelings and that I congratulate him on his full submission." At the same time, the pope approved the two proposals made by Father Lagrange: devoting the *Revue biblique* to Palestinian studies, taking a year's leave, "starting when he himself proposes it, without rancor."

Father Lagrange did not know that Father Cormier had already communicated this first letter of submission to Pope Pius X. He felt he should proclaim his obedience to the pope, while professing his loyalty. On August 17, he wrote directly to Pope Pius X.

Most Holy Father,

Prostrate at the feet of Your Holiness, I come to affirm my sorrow at having saddened you and my entire obedience. My first act was, and my last one will be, always to submit my mind and spirit, wholeheartedly, to the orders of the vicar of Jesus Christ. Precisely because I feel I have the heart of a most obedient son, please permit me to tell you, Father, the Most August of Fathers, yet a Father, the sorrow I feel at seeing the reprobation attached to several of my works whose titles are not listed as though they were tainted with rationalism. I am quite ready to recognize that those works may contain some errors, but that they were written in a spirit of disobedience to church tradition or to the decisions of the Pontifical Biblical Commission, Most Holy Father, please permit me to say that nothing was more remote from my mind.

I remain kneeling before Your Holiness to implore your blessing.

> The most humble son of your Holiness,
> brother M. J. Lagrange
> of the Friars Preachers

This time, the pope asked the master general to make the document public in the press, which would show to the eyes of all with what disposition Father Lagrange had received the prescriptions of the Holy See. On September 5, Father Cormier notified Father Lagrange of his news: "I was received in audience yesterday by the Holy Father, who spontaneously expressed his great and full satisfaction with your letter, encouraging me to publish it. I added that you had been distressed that some had said you were a rationalist and not submissive. Your wish, on the contrary, had been to safeguard the veracity, even the historical truth of the Old Testament, and what you wrote in that sense is far earlier than the recent decisions."

Father Lagrange had also made an act of allegiance to the Biblical Commission. Its president, Cardinal Rampolla, had always held him in esteem and trusted him. He answered on September 12: "I knew well your noble virtues, which I have always appreciated and valued. Now, your letter declaring your complete submission to the wishes of the Holy Father is a new proof of your qualities as an excellent religious, and it does you credit. God will no doubt bless your intentions and your efforts. He will especially protect your new work, and you will have the satisfaction of having worked generously for the glory of the Lord."

Father Lagrange adopted a rule of absolute discretion before his departure from Jerusalem and kept it in Paris, where he was to live for a year. His farewell to the school was brief. "No bitterness and no weakness! No soldier worthy of the name will discuss the order that throws him into battle, still less will he flinch or desert. My prayer and my heart will always be with you, but do not count anymore on my help, for you certainly know that I could not give it to you without being disloyal, even if I did so indirectly and without putting myself forward. If God wants this foundation to live, he will make it live as he did in the past, but you will only deserve his help if you remain brave, enthusiastic, particularly true, religious, dutiful sons of the order and of the church in your hearts and in your minds." The only traces we have of his distress come from fleeting confidences to his friend Xavier Faucher: "I am no longer but a wreck, at the orders of the master general. I am leaving for France on September 3....I am on a year's leave, approved by the Holy Father...wonderful goodwill of the young. In a great hurry, abrupt departure, my heart would fail if I were to linger," he wrote from Jerusalem on September 1. From Roybon, on September 22, he wrote: "I think I did my best to serve the church through my action. The time has come to serve it through inaction, and all is well, if one has something to suffer." From Paris, in October, he confided, "I have not settled down to any work. What can I do in this turmoil?"

Father Lagrange appeared in public only to preach the Advent sermons in the Church of St. Séverin. He spoke the first Sunday on devotion to the pope, concluding in a way that received favorable notice in the newspapers. "We must love the pope. We, especially the French, could not obey, if we did not love. Sons of Celts, we know how to give our all; we don't know how to mark time. If the pope tempers our efforts, if he orders us not to advance when our generosity urges us to go forward, that is our trial. We shall overcome it, if we really love the pope. Were he to say to his soldiers—'You are useless in battle. Go. Guard the baggage!'—we would do so with joy." Father Lagrange echoed here the instructions he gave his disciples on leaving Jerusalem.

Once the decree of the Consistorial had been promulgated in Rome on August 16, the press had taken up the matter. On the side of the strictest traditionalists in France, *L'univers* made the most out of the decree, both by centering it on Father Lagrange and by overvaluing its meaning. The way that the decree was formulated made it seem that it was first written for the Diocese of Paderborn against the book written by Dr. Holzhey, that another book by the German Fritz Tillman had been added to it, and that, for good measure, the *plura scripta* of Father Lagrange had been inserted between the two. The insertion had taken place during the final stage of editing, somewhat fortuitously, in this context. Who inserted them? As long as the archives of the Holy See, where one might find the answer, still remain closed, no hypothesis may be offered. Already, on August 23, *L'univers* had published an article by Roger Duguet (Father Paul Boulin), titled "The School Index of the Consistorial."

> A debate is going on today in some circles about a new decree, forbidding the use of the books by Father Lagrange, the exegete of the School of Jerusalem, well known as a hypercritic. All good Catholics, who know the harm done by these works to the young clergy and the profit some ecclesiastical writers draw from them in this country, men like Labourt, Hemmer, and others, will rejoice at the news. There is talk about underhand maneuvers tending to elude this decree....The Consistorial, up until now, far from going back on its judgment, seems, on the contrary, to have committed other Vatican departments to greater severity....Were these wise judgments to be opposed, were a revision to be asked for, the only result would probably be to make the penalty more severe, and that kind of appeal is usually fatal to those who appeal.

On Saturday, September 28, *L'univers* repeated its accusation in an article entitled "The Lagrange Case," publishing and commenting on Father Lagrange's letter to the Pope. "Some of the learned exegete's works, and more particularly, his theory on the author of the Pentateuch, had been submitted to the examination of the Supreme Congregation as upholding suspect doctrine and tendencies....Though he may have gone too far or even erred on certain questions, his intentions, at least, were pure, and he was the victim of the rationalistic and hypercritical spirit of German Protestant authors, so widespread nowadays in the world of biblical exegesis, rather than its accomplice." Emmanuel Barbier in *La critique du liberalisme* of October 1, went even further, calling the disciplinary measure taken by the Consistorial a "dogmatic decree" against the "errors" of Father Lagrange.

The liberal current, principally represented by Maurice Pernot in *Le journal des débats* and by Pierre Imbart de la Tour in the *Bulletin de la semaine*, and also by Julien de Narfon in *Le figaro*, presented the intervention of the Consistorial as a side effect of the foundation of the Biblical Institute in Rome and as a result of maneuvers against the Biblical School by [the institute] chairman, Leopold Fonck. As Father Jaussen explained on September 23 to the minister of Foreign Affairs, the Dominicans in Jerusalem were convinced that "the decision taken in regard to Lagrange was inspired in Rome by Fonck, a German Jesuit, who directs biblical studies in Rome, and who tried, unsuccessfully, in 1911, to establish in Jerusalem a biblical school competing with that of the Dominicans." The journalists would speculate for several months on the themes of political maneuvers and religious rivalry. Rumors that Germany sought to supplant the French presence in the Near East and that the Jesuits of the Biblical Institute in Rome were preferred by the pope to the Dominicans of the Biblical School in Jerusalem had been current since 1909 when the Biblical Institute was founded by Pope Pius X. A few lines in the editorial appearing in the *Bulletin de la semaine*, September 25, indicated they proposed a campaign on behalf of Father

Lagrange. Intrigues lay behind the decree of the Consistorial, they reported. "We have known about these intrigues for a year. Father Lagrange himself asked us not to say anything about them. Scholar of integrity and remarkable religious that he is, the director of the Biblical School had faith in the truth and the approval of his superiors for his defense. The Consistorial, through its official examiners, judged otherwise. The government and public opinion are warned. We hope the Biblical School will be saved. But it is good that certain 'Roman circles' know that we are not taken in by the reasons they give to try to destroy it." This intervention by the *Bulletin de la semaine* in defense of the Biblical School and Father Lagrange earned the publication of a condemnation by the church. The condemnation was issued by Cardinal Andrieu in April 1913, and corroborated by Cardinal Merry del Val on April 23 and by Cardinal de Laï on June 5. Sixty French bishops publicly approved it. The *Bulletin* would never recover.

A severe controversy, which was to flare up again in 1913, was already growing between journalists and Jesuits. Father Fonck responded through an intermediary. Father Cavallera responded anonymously. Father Dudon commented openly. Father Lagrange kept silent. He wrote to the master general on September 15. "I do not think it is opportune to write in order to deny inaccuracies in that article [*Le journal des débats*, September 7]. I can only see salvation in silence, absolute silence. Were I to write once to a newspaper, I would have to begin again. Whatever I did not refute would be considered to come from me. I would be lost." Father Lagrange's resolve grew stronger as the controversy broadened. "As for articles in the press, I already had the honor to tell you that I had nothing to do with the article in *Débats*....I repeat to anyone willing to listen to me that the Holy Father was only guided by the purest motives of faith. Do you wish me to intervene publicly to put things straight? That I cannot believe," he wrote on October 22. Again, on November 21, he gave his assurance: "Let me assure you that I foment no agitation in Paris." By December 16, he was becoming agitated: "I need not tell you that I have nothing whatever to do with the notes in the newspapers, be they rightist or leftist. I saw neither Mr. de Narfon nor anybody belonging to *Débats*....I also know nothing about what is going on in Rome on this subject. And I can even keep my peace!" Yet, public opinion, at least that part of it which sought not to oppose church tradition to modern knowledge, remained deeply troubled by the disavowal the Holy See had inflicted upon the work of one of its most faithful servants.

Chapter VIII

FROM REPROBATION
TO RECONCILIATION

Thanks to Father Lagrange's public submission, the Index spared him. Although he would have sacrificed *La méthode historique* to save *St. Mark*, he wasn't called upon to make that choice. Neither his *St. Mark* nor *La méthode historique* was condemned. The *Revue biblique*, with the express agreement of the pope, would remain unchanged and continue to deal with holy scripture instead of being confined to Near Eastern archaeology. Better still, with regard to Pope Pius X, Father Lagrange's situation would be happily clarified. No longer would he be perceived by the pope as Loisy's accomplice.

Although Pope Pius X had received Father Lagrange with kindness in March 1905, his associations with Pope Leo XIII and Cardinal Rampolla were known, and he soon fell suspect. As the provincial of the Dominicans in Paris wrote to Father Cormier on June 28, 1907: "We all suffer at the thought that the Holy Father holds us all more or less under suspicion because of Father Lagrange's teachings." To Father Lagrange on June 29, 1909, Father Cormier wrote: "Your moral credit has been affected because the Holy Father views you with some suspicion, and the public largely shares this suspicion." The pope sought the aide of trustworthy men, and he did not always feel sure of finding them among the Dominicans. He occasionally made harsh remarks about Father Lagrange or the Biblical School, and his words were repeated. On September 1906, Father Cormier, gave this report. "The Holy Father tells me: 'In this matter be hard; you can be sure that the Holy See will stand by you.'" Father Lagrange's commentary on Genesis was prohibited. It is an order "that the Holy Father confirmed, speaking to me yesterday," Father Cormier wrote on June ll, 1907. He left no doubt about who was responsible for this prohibition.

Sometimes Father Cormier's orders were milder, but these orders concerned Fribourg rather than Jerusalem. "The Holy Father asked me to proceed cautiously, though I should endeavor to put things straight," he wrote on July 1, 1907. The Holy Father thought that Father Lagrange was being manipulated by enemies of the church. "'At bottom, they exploit us.' That is what the Holy Father told me [Cormier] a few days ago relating to a nasty business in which a priest was taking refuge behind Father Lagrange" (February 9, 1908). At the Vatican, it was well known that the direction of the Biblical School did not coincide with that advocated by Pope Pius X. Cormier kept Lagrange aware of events as they unfolded. "He [the pope] does not think that they are delighted with what he does in Jerusalem, nor are they in a hurry to help him efficiently *con amore*" (April 22, 1908). "There is a rumor spreading among some of our fathers that certain professors remain tacitly silent, awaiting better days and foreseeing that, if they were unlucky enough to raise unfavorable opinions, the pope would strike pitilessly *quod est inconveniens*" (June 18, 1909). "Some witty remarks are repeated....That some of those words may have reached the Holy Father, I have no proof. But the other day, Monday, June 21, as we were speaking of these things, he spoke to me about you: 'Right now there is nothing, but there is the past' " (June 28, 1909).

In front of third parties other than Father Cormier, the pope was just as harsh. The bishop of Grenoble, in February 1908, heard him say of Father Lagrange: "Sometimes he limps," and was struck by the severity of the tone. In June 1909, the pope made another declaration to the archbishop of Orléans: "We must fear he will not change unless he feels the iron hand of the Holy See!" On April 4, 1907, the second time Father Lagrange was received in audience by Pope Pius X, along with the members of the Commission for Studies in the Dominican Order, the pope showed a stern attitude. "When my name was called, he asked: '*Come stanno a Gerusalemme?*' and that was all."

Yet Father Lagrange was never heard to say a bitter or irreverent word against Pope Pius X. While his own disciples did not refrain from being ironic, an area where Monsignor Duchesne remained unsurpassed, Father Lagrange, in his conversation and in his teachings, showed the greatest respect for the acts of the Holy See. The only thing one could reproach him with was having said: "The pope is not a scholar." He never bargained his obedience or even his defense. "How could you believe," he complained to Father Cormier, "that I disapproved the condemnations coming from His Holiness Pope Pius X?" What could he have done to seem less blameworthy without pretending he had joined the conservative camp? Writing his *Personal Reflections and Memoirs* in 1926, Father Lagrange wondered, "Can one justify oneself against suspicion of hypocrisy? When I think of how kindly the pope received my submission in 1912, I believe that if I had sent him then [in 1909] a filial letter, opening my heart more completely than I had ever done before, his suspicions might perhaps have faded away."

"He who excuses himself, accuses himself." Guided by this axiom, Father Cormier advised Father Lagrange not to justify himself before the public or even before the Consistorial Congregation. Father Lagrange, therefore, did not plead his case against the accusations of the Consistorial decree.

Things had flared up again when the Consistorial, purporting to answer a question posed by the archbishop of Siena, indicated which of Father Lagrange's works were being aimed at by the Consistorial decree. There is, however, no record in Siena or in Rome of the archbishop's correspondence. The Consistorial reprimand, dated October 1912, printed in November in the official bulletin of the Diocese of Siena, fell into public hands in mid-December and only came to the attention of the master general at that time. With its publication, Father Lagrange's position worsened considerably.

Among Father Lagrange's works, the following were cleared: the tomes on the *Études sur les religions semitiques* (published in 1903, reissued in 1905), *Le messianisme chez les juifs* (1909), the short publications taken from the *Revue biblique*—*Ancient Crete* (1908), *A Few Remarks on the "Orpheus" of Solomon Reinach* (1910), the publications that remained confidential, *Éclaircissement...* (1905), and *Genesis* (1906). How did his works offend the Holy See? Three reproaches concerned the procedures of the *Revue biblique*, three basic criticisms dealt with biblical hermeneutics. Specifically, the *Revue* exercised a disastrous influence on the younger clergy, leading it to welcome the critical interpretation of the Bible, and inspiring it with respect for unbelieving scholarship. Furthermore, it was not evenhanded between the representatives of modern exegesis, which it praised, and the defenders of Catholic tradition, on which it poured contempt, especially when they were hostile to liberal ideals; it called upon collaborators suspect because of their ideas, some of whom had even renounced the faith. As to the hermeneutics advocated or practiced by Lagrange, the indictment censured him on three points. It censured his doctrine on the inspiration of the holy books which made the truth relative to whatever was written therein and even admitted the presence of errors in profane manners. It censured his conception of biblical narratives that reduced or even suppressed their historical truth, for instance, the story of Lot's wife. It censured his theory of the literary composition of biblical texts that admitted the presence of different sources in the holy Books, that moved back the traditionally admitted dates, that suppressed the paternity of the author they are named after. Such were, in brief, the reasons put forth for the reprimand against Lagrange on June 29, 1912.

What was Father Lagrange to do under these circumstances? As always, he would accept. He sought to explain himself to the master general:

A new opportunity to examine myself is provided by the explanations given by the Consistorial Congregation to his excellency, the archbishop of Siena. As to this I must declare that I have never nor do I today have the intention of protesting against this measure to which I have very respectfully submitted....Secondly, I declare that I am resolved not to undertake anything that resembles a discussion with the Consistorial Congregation. I know my duty with regard to authority, and I shall fulfill it. So, if such a discussion were to start in the newspapers, I would not be involved in it. But I think I can give you, my Most Reverend Father, some explanations that might be useful to you and that could, should the occasion arise, be presented to the supreme authority, with all the deference and respect we owe it, if that authority should express the wish to hear the accused.

As to the reprimand of the *Revue biblique*, it was not Father Lagrange's fault if scholarship in philology, history, and geography progressed mainly through the work of non-Catholic academics. "This situation, so impressive to young clerics, is not due to the *Revue biblique*." The *Revue* never hesitated in contesting what was questionable in their publications; it did this more effectively as it did it in measured terms. "It cannot be wrong to practice justice toward everyone, as well as that flower of justice that is politeness. The impartiality shown in this way gives but more weight to the criticism that goes with the praise." As to Catholic authors, if the review was viewed as not quite impartial, it was either for not having denounced their shortcomings severely enough, or else because it had preferred to pass over their second-rate work in silence, so as not to appear too unfair. As Father Lagrange had already written in 1904: "Am I too proud? Yet, it seems to me that I hear this cry of the church that we should not be taken for simpletons who can only heap praises upon each other." Some of the collaborators of the *Revue* had apostatized [given up the faith]. "This point is the most painful for me, since it touches those who have honored me by collaborating in the *Revue biblique*. I deplore the fact that some of them had the misfortune to lose their faith, but what review, unless it is run by a prophet, can be safe from such a misfortune?"

Father Lagrange responded to several questions concerning his doctrinal approach. Might not there be some errors in the Bible? "If these errors are formal, that is, if they treat of things that have been erroneously asserted or denied by the sacred author (when he is not speaking according to appearances), I have always answered by distinguishing the range of those statements according to their literary genre: *strict history, primitive history, edifying history*, and others." Secondly, are the biblical narratives devoid of historical truth? First of all, the aim of the Bible is not to tell the history of the world. In that respect, it shows enormous gaps. Furthermore, some biblical narratives may only have the appearance of history. In these areas, the exegetes should give their interpretations freely within the limits granted by the Biblical Commission. "I have expressly refused to call any part of the Bible *myth*....But I would lie if I said that I considered the episode of Lot's wife changing into a pillar of salt strictly historical. This is a particular case for exegesis." Next, has criticism the right to elucidate the literary composition of biblical texts? "Subject to the points decided by the authority of the church, there is here a space for free opinions, to be debated among Catholics. Let each one prove his competence to deal with them."

Father Lagrange's memorandum provided the opportunity for him to explain once more his attitude toward the instructions given by the Holy See.

> I know quite well that we must always be perfectly obedient to the present superior who is given us by God, and that he can change the directions given by his predecessor, especially if he is the supreme head of the church. I was thus ready to obey Pope Pius X, as I had

obeyed Pope Leo XIII. Was I not to notice that my works were not agreeable? Let me be quite honest. Yes, I was, so I thought it was my duty to write to His Holiness to declare that I would immediately give up the study of scripture, if such was his wish. His Holiness was so good as to show his satisfaction at my attitude, without adding anything else. Thus, I thought that I was allowed to continue. I thought that if Pope Pius X was personally inclined toward certain ideas, he considered it advisable, as supreme head of the church, to let other opinions express themselves, and that is why he said that consultors of the Biblical Commission had been chosen who had different opinions and different methods. I believed those opinions and those methods could be compatible with orthodoxy. I did not think the measure taken by the Sacred Congregation established the contrary. But, as you understood from the very first day, and as the Holy Father deigned to agree, the measure dissuades me from any longer dealing with biblical studies, at least as long as the question of orthodoxy has not been settled.

There were to be no more biblical studies as long as Father Lagrange's orthodoxy remained in question. He held firmly to his resolve. "I can assure you that I only look for peace and quiet, that I avoid speaking of biblical questions or even thinking of them…. It has been decided from the beginning, with the Holy Father's agreement, that I personally should no longer deal with biblical studies." The commentary on the Gospel of Luke that he had begun after his Mark commentary and of which he had already written three chapters by April 1912 was not to come out until 1921. During his first exile in Paris, Father Lagrange did not deal with exegesis but with archaeology and history. He had studied Greece and Persia and carefully examined the trophies brought back to the Louvre from the excavations at Susa. He had written a study on Marcus Aurelius. His list of publications during the year 1913 verifies this. When Lagrange did return to the exegesis of the New Testament, he would not continue the commentary on the gospels as long as there remained the slightest doubt about the orthodoxy of his *St. Mark*. Instead, he would start a study of St. Paul, writing commentaries on his epistles to the Romans and to the Galatians. Who knows if a new ecclesiastical censure would not have led him to comment on the Book of Revelation, after having gone from Genesis to Mark and from Mark to Paul? Others, paralyzed by similar shackles, had turned to safer studies, when they did not forsake the field of scholarly research altogether. Not so, Father Lagrange.

"How I would like to go back to Jerusalem!" This leitmotif reappears continuously in the letters Father Lagrange wrote from France from 1912 to 1913. "I am not necessary for St. Stephen but St. Stephen is necessary for me, so that I can work. My wish is to stay there, except for my vow of obedience." This wish, first voiced in 1903, remained unchanged. A month had hardly gone by, when Father Lagrange suggested: "Once everything has been settled, since the Holy Father was pleased with my submission, so they say, could I not finish my vacation in Jerusalem, without teaching, of course?...My wish would be therefore to go back to my cell, to the divine office in choir and to all the convent life I cherish so much," he wrote on October 5, 1912. Father Cormier considered his request premature; it meant shifting about too soon. Father Lagrange responded on October 12, "I understand quite well that I cannot go back at once to Jerusalem." He appealed on November 1. "I am still quite ready to return to Jerusalem." A little later the revolution of the Young Turks had caused a turmoil in Palestine. "I wonder if the serious events in Turkey could not be a reason for sending me back to Jerusalem....My long experience in that country and my age might perhaps enable me to be of some use to our fathers. In the end, I am at your disposal," he wrote on January 26, 1913. But the leave he had been granted was to last for one year. "I cannot leave

Paris before the end of June. After that, I hope I shall at last be allowed to go back *al dolce nido,*" he confided on May 10, 1913. "I feel a little ill at ease outside the priory, and I wish for nothing better than to go back to Jerusalem. Can I count upon going home at the beginning of July?" Father Lagrange missed the atmosphere of religious life—which had been suppressed in France at the time of the expulsions—at least as much as the environment of scholarly research.

Dated June 5, the register of the general curia of the order carried an offhand mention: "Lagrange, Paris, may go back to Jerusalem. He must resume his course on exegesis; he is praised for his intention of studying St. Paul's epistles." Father Lagrange's *Personal Reflections and Memoirs* are no clearer about this sudden reconciliation that put an end to his exile. The only relevant account we have of it is the one left by Father Hugues Vincent, always a confidant, in his "Life of Father Lagrange," which remains unpublished. During an interview when Pope Pius X asked incidentally how Father Lagrange was faring, the master general was very glad to be able to say that the director of the Biblical School, having left Jerusalem at the beginning of the previous September, was now in Paris engaged in apostolic ministry while pursuing religious studies that were extraneous to the Bible itself. The pope, pleased with such total and filial obedience, stated that Father Lagrange was to be sent back at once to his school and to his interrupted biblical works, but that he wished to see him first. A telegram from the general curia summoned Father Lagrange hastily to Rome without providing any explanation. A few hours after having received this message, Father Lagrange was on his way. The process was enough to trouble even the most hardened warrior. "I am leaving for Rome," wrote Father Lagrange to his disciples in Jerusalem, "called most urgently by the master general, with no other indication. It may be that I shall have to give certain explanations in person, though that is hardly the custom. So, it is much more likely that I will be notified directly of the doctrinal condemnation that so many voices have already predicted, and to which I have already submitted. Do not tell anybody around you before you get precise news, which will be sent as soon as possible. In any case, I ask our Lord and his dear mother to inspire you with the attitude and the feeling of real sons of obedience, whatever happens."

When Father Lagrange arrived in Rome, he asked for some explanation as to his lot. Wishing him to have the spiritual benefit of his ordeal right to the end, Father Cormier, according to Father Vincent, simply told him that the Holy Father would give him his instructions during an audience that was already set for two days later, in the morning. The period seemed long, the waiting painful to Father Lagrange. For two days, he prepared himself by praying and recollection to receive the severest sentence. The day arrived. No sooner had he been shown in and begun the formal salutations than he was moved to hear the Holy Father invite him in a fatherly way to come closer. The pope congratulated him on his loyal and prompt submission to the church, and for his obedience to the wishes of his superior. Then the pope urged him to take up teaching once again as director of the Biblical School of Jerusalem, while remaining in the same submissive spirit. Finally, he blessed him and all his collaborators. The only thing left for Father Lagrange was to go back to Paris to prepare for his return to Jerusalem.

For Father Lagrange, as for his friends, after a time of reprobation, came the time of reconciliation. Monsignor Batiffol also benefited from a measure of grace for his *Eucharistie*, which had been condemned by decree on July 26, 1903, and publicly placed on the Index on January 2, 1911. A newly corrected version had just been authorized. "I think that this favor shown me," Father Batiffol declared, "goes further than my humble self, and that positive theology, in general, will benefit from it. The return of Father Lagrange to Jerusalem, decided in the same week, permits one to think that our group, the group using the historical method, has overcome the prejudice that was still so violent a year ago. I believe, on the other hand, that the group of immanence is [still] at the heart of the tempest. Cardinal Billot is at work on it himself. Cardinal Amette told me so formally last Saturday" (June 10, 1913). Indeed, on June 17, two of Father Laberthonnière's works were put on the Index. [The group of immanence were some French Catholic thinkers who were trying to integrate elements of Kantian idealist philosophy.]

A family duty delayed Father Lagrange's return to Jerusalem by a few days. His nephew Albert, an officer in Morocco, the son of Pauline Lagrange and Vincent Rambaud, had been killed in an ambush on January 16, during the pacification of the Rif. His body was to be returned home for burial at Roybon on July 2. His coffin did not arrive in Marseille until July 3, however. Father Lagrange met it and accompanied it.

The next day, after the funeral, Father Lagrange went back to Marseille, embarked on July 5, and arrived in Jerusalem on July 12 in the morning. The prior of St. Stephen had come to meet him at Jaffa. Father Lagrange felt gratified. "I have been back here for two days," he wrote on July 14 to Father Hyvernat, "and I must tell you how sorry I was not to have been able to wait for you in France. Quite unexpectedly, the master general asked me to go back to Jerusalem, and I thought I should not dawdle....Despite the heat, I am glad to be back in a priory where one leads the Dominican life of choir and studies, in what may be a rather excessive solitude, but...better than the life without any religious home that one must lead in France." The Dominican brethren were filled with a joy the prior had mentioned in writing to the master general on July 19. "I must thank you once more for the return of Père Lagrange. We are so happy to have him in our midst!" As for his closest disciple, Father Hugues Vincent, he confided a few months later to a friend at the Biblical School: "On July 12, it was quite sure. My master [Father Lagrange] was here. We were at once speaking about the church, truth, work, calmly and enthusiastically, as we used to do twenty years before when all was smiling on our hope."

The press only learned about Father Lagrange's return after he had embarked for Jerusalem. In the *Bulletin de la semaine* that had been so passionate in defending the Biblical School and its director, the information was limited to a short news item. "Our readers know how, after certain incidents, Father Lagrange, obeying the instructions of his superiors, had left the Biblical School of Jerusalem. We are pleased to learn that his disfavor has come to an end. On the order of Father Cormier, the master general of the Dominicans, the learned exegete has left for Jerusalem, where he will take up again, along with his teaching, the research work that has won for him a rightful authority in the scholarly world."

Had all the clouds lifted? Perhaps, not yet. "I do not know how my case stands in Rome," wrote Lagrange to Hyvernat on November 16. "I understood, through a letter from the master general, that nothing was finished. The question may be brought back for discussion any day. It is true there are many others. Yet, nonetheless, my mind is not quite at ease....I act as if it were, and I work." At the Biblical School itself life was back to normal. On Christmas Eve 1913, Father Vincent wrote up a report. "During the last six months, Father Lagrange has done as much work as he would have done in thirty years, and that, in spite of numerous difficulties. The school is working with only one foreign student and four young Dominicans from different provinces, and all is going as well with five students as with fifty."

The calm did not last. Political events of 1913 and 1914 would create a year of deferments. On August 4, 1914, Father Lagrange himself noted in the house chronicle: "No solemn celebration for St. Dominic. Fathers Vincent, Abel, Petitot, Dhorme, Carrière are leaving [for military duty]. Long live France! Let victory be ours!" During that month of August, the last Dominicans able to bear arms went back to their countries. In December, the Turks arrested and deported all Frenchmen who remained in Jerusalem. As tragedy impended, on December 14, Father Lagrange wrote his farewell to Father Vincent with overwhelming emotion:

My Son,

I will most probably be leaving for Orfa, the ancient Edessa, blessed city. You will learn about the circumstances. I am writing to you, not knowing whether you are still alive, and thinking rather that you are dead, so, only to tell you, if you are still alive, that I keep thinking of you with the same affection in God, and that I always commend you to the Holy Virgin Mary with the same trust. She has presided over our friendship and over the many prayers we have said together, kneeling at her feet.

I have read the pages you wrote before you left. Thank you. I, too, ask God to keep me brave and pure.

Be sure that, if I come to die, my last earthly thoughts will be for you.

I do not want to live in the New World that is being born. We are going back to barbarous times by the use of science without God. Who will, from now on, find interest in our innocent studies?

Yet, intelligence will perhaps recover its rights again, and it will be necessary for the church to be given at last the solution to the biblical questions that have been raised. If I have been mistaken, you know it was in good faith. As I know your intention is as straight as mine and your submission is the same as mine, I ask you not to despair of the task to which we have given our lives in such harmony of thought and, on your part, such total abnegation as to your personal interest.

Before leaving, I have gone over every corner of our dear St. Stephen's. I have accomplished my *tristesse d'Olympio*, but it changed into thanksgiving when I remembered all the happiness we experienced by serving God in that solitude, by working for what we considered the honor of the church, the good of souls, the kingdom of Jesus Christ, Our Savior. Your friendship was for me strength and joy; often, also, a source of acute suffering, but all is well as it is.

Farewell, my son, I hold you tenderly in Jesus Christ, Our Lord.

Your Father,
M. J. Lagrange
of the Friars Preachers

On that very evening, the fate of the Biblical School was sealed. Until the end of World War I, only the Swiss lay brothers and Father Doumeth, of Lebanese origin, would stay on. One of the Swiss, Brother Martin Grillet, recounted in his diary what happened to Father Lagrange and his companions. On December 14, at 9:00 p.m., the French Dominicans of St. Stephen were arrested by the Turkish police and taken to Damascus under guard. They arrived there on the night of December 17 or 18, supervised by the police. After Pope Benedict XV had intervened to try to prevent them from being deported to Orfa, they were taken by train from Damascus to Beirut, still escorted by the police. They arrived there on December 22 and were kept under arrest for four days. "On the evening of December 26, we embarked on the *Scylla:* three hundred religious and nuns crammed on the deck, in the rain, without a tarpaulin drawn over our heads. The sea was rough, and soon a storm came up that would grow more violent, raging for three nights and two days. We were drenched by waves sweeping the deck, tossing us against one another and keeping us in water day and night. On December 29, in the morning, we put in at Rhodes. In the evening, the sea grew calmer. We left again toward Piraeus, where we arrived on December 30, at 8:00 p.m." From there, two days later, they embarked for Brindisi on the *Milano*, where they arrived on January 3. On January 4, they celebrated Mass at a shrine in Pompei. At last, late in the evening on January 5, they arrived in Rome. Brother Martin was probably not the only one in the state he depicted: "Sick, exhausted, cold, full of rheumatic pains!" In Rome, Lagrange is eagerly received by Benediet XV on January 8, 1915.

At the head of the church, a corner had been turned. Two weeks after the beginning of World War I, on August 20, 1914, Pope Pius X had died. In his stead, Cardinal Giacomo della Chiesa had been elected pope. Cardinal della Chiesa had formerly worked with Cardinal Rampolla at the Secretariat. Pope Pius X had sent him to Bologna in 1907. He had been made a *cardinal in extremis* on March 25, 1914. Everything allowed one to expect that once he had become Pope Benedict XV, he would break with the tendency of his predecessor. Yet, for several years, other priorities were to mobilize his energies, so that the doctrinal questions raised by the study of the Bible would only come back to the foreground once the roar of arms had died.

Chapter IX

THE MODERNIST CRISIS: AFTERMATH

The École Biblique after the First World War

During the war, the Spanish consul, as well as Father Doumeth, who was Lebanese, and the lay brothers, who were Swiss, protected St. Stephen priory in Jerusalem. Their presence had prevented the priory from being ransacked, and they were able to save the library. As none of the professors who were mobilized as soldiers had been killed in battle and as Father Abel had been only slightly wounded, the future of the École biblique seemed positive.

"The Practical School of Biblical Studies was closed because it was French; it will come back to life as French." With these proud words, Father Lagrange ended his article in the *Revue biblique* on May 1915. The question, however, remained: Could the school be brought back to life again? Jerusalem was liberated by the English at the beginning of December 1917. The rout of the Turkish army was completed in September 1918. It then became possible to consider moving back to Jerusalem. Father Lagrange made a hurried trip to Rome in September 1918 to ask for the authority to reopen the school. Then, invited by the British delegate for the provisional settlement of the Near East question, he sailed on a British torpedo boat from Taranto to Port Said, from November 7 to 11. On November 12, he was back in Jerusalem after having been away for forty-seven months. As soon as its professors were demobilized, the school would be able to take up teaching activities again. Its staff, the library, and the buildings had been left untouched. Although there was only one student, Joseph Chaine, for the school year 1919 to 1920, the school would again open, and the future seemed brighter.

In the church a new page had been turned. The savage repression of Modernism was followed by a soothing period of decompression. The intellectual climate had been tempered by the cultural gap caused by war, by the accession of a moderate prelate to the Roman See, and by the dissolution of the *Sodalicium pianum,* an incriminatory enterprise sometimes known as *La sapinière* or "the Fir-tree Plantation." The war had thinned the number of researchers. On the other hand, Father Louis Venard explained: "It has at least brightened the atmosphere that had been troubled by the Modernist crisis...the necessary work of Catholic criticism, which Father Lagrange and his friends had initiated under somewhat difficult circumstances, can now continue in peace and confidence for the greatest profit of true scholarship and the good name of French Catholicism."

At the school, continuity seemed guaranteed and the relief team assured. Indeed, none was missing among the young professors Father Lagrange had taught. Among them, Father Dhorme was to become the new head of the school. "I am no longer but the past," wrote Father Lagrange in 1922. "He [Father Dhorme] can be a very important instrument for the future." Elected prior of St. Stephen in April 1919, reelected in 1922, Father Dhorme was appointed director of the École biblique and editor of the *Revue biblique* in 1923. Furthermore, in the days to come, the school finally would receive official status. As early as 1919, the British archaeologist John Garstang, a professor at Liverpool University, had invited the Biblical School to enter, as a French partner, with Great Britain and the United States in a learned body dedicated to the archaeological research affecting Palestine. Consequently, the Academy of Inscriptions and Literature, after having deliberated on October 15, 1920, "considers that St.

Stephen Biblical School through its organization, its scientific situation and its authority, is naturally designated to become the French Archaeological School in Jerusalem, and entrusts its correspondent, Father Lagrange, with the task of seeing to it that France obtains the part which should be hers in the study of Palestinian antiquities, in scientific agreement with the English and American schools."

Seeing the scholarly work of the school officially honored, Father Lagrange might rightly have rejoiced had the esteem shown by the French authorities not been in painful contrast to the persistent suspicion shown by Rome. He could not help deploring the discrepancy that he felt was detrimental to the school. "Here we are, the French archaeological school, officially acknowledged both by our government and by the mandatory power, forming a consortium with the Americans. It is a very great success, one that I would never have thought possible at the outset. It is true that I expected to get a kindly reception from Rome, but we must know that we are not really in great favor there. As I am, above all, a son of the church, I shall only find solace in a clear approval from the Holy See. [For now,] I am obliged to be content with good memories from the time of Pope Leo XIII."

In the years immediately following the war, the Biblical School was still suspected, and often threatened by Rome. It was, however, staunchly defended by the Dominican master general. With a new crisis looming on the horizon, the school became the target of suspicion and blame once more, and the struggle to prove its innocence resumed.

Suspicion and Threat

The mistrust of the Holy See for the school reared its head once more in May 1909 when the Biblical Institute was founded in Rome. Pope Leo XIII had called upon Father Lagrange to create in Rome a Center of Biblical Studies offering a pluralism similar to that which had led to the choice of the forty consultants of the Biblical Commission as it was first envisaged. Now, Pope Pius X had entrusted the foundation to the Jesuit Father Fonck. Father Fonck was well known as an opponent of Father Lagrange and as an exegete hostile to the historical-critical method. He was a zealous supporter of the more and more restrictive interpretation dictated by the new Biblical Commission; moreover, the law organizing the new institute set it up as a Jesuit fiefdom. Its president was to be appointed by the Supreme Pontiff on the proposal of the Jesuit superior general, while the full professors would be nominated by the superior general, with the agreement of the Holy See.

Inevitably, the Biblical Institute in Rome and the Biblical School in Jerusalem would become antagonistic. The difference was marked. One school had been founded by the Dominican Order and had no official status in the church. The second had been entrusted to the Jesuits and had been established as a Pontifical Institution by Rome. Some observers saw in the establishment of a Pontifical Institution a defeat inflicted upon Father Lagrange. Indeed, Father Fonck's aggressive behavior soon justified their apprehension. Strengthened by the authority with which the pope had invested him, sure of the doctrinal line he was to impose inside the church, he embarked upon a *crusade* against the Biblical School of Jerusalem.

Before courses had even begun at the institute, Father Lagrange could foresee difficulties. As early as August 1909, he had commented: "If, in relation to Rome, we are viewed as a kind of practical school, all will be well....To say the truth, I would be very surprised if the [Jesuit] fathers did not take advantage of the favorable wind to found a biblical school in Jerusalem itself." During his courses, the president of the Pontifical Institute, Father Fonck, poured venom upon the exegetes of the "broad school." He was noted as having said, "Once the Jerusalem Biblical School and the [Catholic] universities of Paris, Louvain, and Fribourg have been destroyed, then some progress can be made in a Catholic direction!" The professors of the Biblical

School, for their part, had to show plenty of irony not to be out-done. More serious were the plans to set up a branch of the Roman institute in the Holy Land. The first offensive [in the view of this foundation] began as far back as June 1911. It was to be founded in Palestine on Mount Carmel. In August of the same year, Father Fonck warmly recommended to the Patriarch of Jerusalem by the Secretary of State, left for the Holy Land to pre-pare the foundation. During his stay, he spread shattering decla-rations against Father Lagrange. "I will break his back," he boasted everywhere. As for Father Lagrange, he was sure that Father Fonck, "asking for an egg so as to get an ox," was aiming at Jerusalem in order to supplant the Biblical School.

In fact, since the Carmelites did not want the presence of the Jesuits on Mount Carmel, Father Fonck's second offensive in May 1912 *was* aimed at Jerusalem. The city was much better suited to the unsurpassable dignity of the Pontifical Institute's struggle against the baneful influence of the Biblical School of Jerusalem. The president of the institute, Father Fonck, refused any kind of amicable negotiation with the Dominicans. On June 29, 1912, Father Lagrange had been publicly blamed by the Consistorial and exiled to Paris for a year, beginning on September 3. Father Fonck took advantage of Father Lagrange's tribulations to speed up the realization of his plan for Jerusalem. His plan was approved by the pope on October 13, and he notified Patriarch Camassei of this approval on the following day. He then obtained, in the name of the pope, French diplomatic protection and arrived in Jerusalem to put his plan in place by Easter 1913. By November, the French press would announce the progressive establishment in Jerusalem of a branch of the Roman institute. Neither the reluctance shown by some Jesuits nor the moves undertaken by the Dominicans could, it seemed, stop the process launched by Father Fonck. Only the First World War deferred his plans.

Why did Father Lagrange stand against the establishment of the institute in Jerusalem? Was he *subjected* to the long-standing rivalry between the Order of Preachers and Friars and the Society of Jesus or *did he reactivate* it? Father Lagrange had always deplored the frictions caused by the *Revue thomiste* and always had told his Jesuit friends, Albert Condamin, Alfred Durand, and Leonce de Grandmaison, that he held no animosity toward them in spite of the open hostility some of its members showed toward him. Did he fear the harm the interests of the Biblical School might suffer through the competition of a similar but rival institution? Certainly, this could be true. If we take into account the many sacrifices he had had to endure to make the Biblical School live, the lack of resources, the lack of books, the lack of qualified collaborators, and the lack of students, he may well have found the rivalry of a Pontifical Institute, powerful in means and in men, threatening. Father Lagrange preferred a harmonious cooperation rather than a violent rivalry that might destroy the Biblical School. He chose to associate the Biblical School with the Roman institute as a school of application. Such collaboration proved impossible, however.

If by the establishment of the Biblical Institute in Jerusalem, the Holy See intended to disavow the Biblical School and, if by the appointment of Jesuits, they sought to counteract the Dominicans' deviation, then St. Stephen school had no choice but to disappear. Such was Father Lagrange's opinion. "This is the most painful point," he explained once he was away from Jerusalem. "It is precisely because I was put under suspicion that the foundation cannot be seen by anybody as [deserving] an act of the Holy See, holding an equal balance between two religious orders....[It] must be considered a mission given to the Jesuits to accomplish, according to their good principles, what the Dominicans have failed to do by following their liberal principles. Here lies the most serious aspect of the question."

The threat of such a disavowal inflicted upon the Biblical School tormented Father Lagrange continuously. In the memorandum he wrote and sent in September 1916 to the new master general, Father Theissling, and again during the steps he undertook in October 1918 with the Roman authorities, his position remained invariable. "I have not got the courage to begin the foundation again," he wrote to Henry Hyvernat on July 16, 1918. "If we go on being treated as suspect, we cannot compete with a Pontifical Institute in Jerusalem. If the Jesuits settle here, we shall only have to withdraw. I mean to say this in Rome, where I am planning to go at the end of September."

Cardinal Van Rossum, the president of the Biblical Commission, who agreed to see Father Lagrange on October 4, did not mince words. To Father Lagrange, who explained his fears concerning the Jesuits, he hinted that the Holy See did not appreciate his lack of submission to the directives imposed by the Biblical Commission. "What you are demanded to do is to follow the direction set by the Holy See. I repeat it once more: What benefit there would be for the church and for your order if you were to conform to it."

Father Lagrange replied with truthfulness. "But it is impossible for me to side with the conservative camp. We refuse to join the camp of rationalism. We cannot adhere to the camp of conservatism. We stand in between. I say it once more. It would be impossible for me to side with conservatism."

The president queried him. "Tell me, Father, to what camp do these decrees belong? In what direction do they point?" "It is obvious that they are conservative." "Such then is the direction imposed by the church, and that it wants it to be followed. A good Catholic acts well when he conforms to it. Such being the premises, such are the conclusions: The foundation in Jerusalem of a school that will follow to the letter the prescribed line flows quite naturally from them."

"With these words I brought the discussion to an end," concluded the cardinal, " and moved to another subject."

The requests presented in Rome by Lagrange ended in a patent failure, according to Jesuit Tacchi Venturi.

Father Lagrange applied to the Congregation of Studies asking that they not authorize the Biblical

Institute to establish a branch in Jerusalem. The Very Reverend Secretary had answered that this did not fall within the competence of the congregation. He [Father Lagrange] also appealed to a cardinal; he must later have felt very sorry that he had done so. The Cardinal praised our project highly and launched a diatribe against the famous Jerusalem *Revue*, a very unreliable periodical as to doctrine, which publishes the answers of the Biblical Commission at the end of the issue, but does not care at all about conforming to them in the preceding pages.

The Biblical School got no encouragement from the Holy See. At least, it was not asked to shut down. Its moral situation under Pope Benedict XV was as precarious as it had been under Pope Pius X. It lived under the constant threat of disavowal; moreover, the twenty-fifth anniversary of the encyclical *Providentissimus Deus* was going to provide an opportunity for new attacks. The orator for the Biblical Institute not only imputed Modernism to the Catholic Institute in Paris and to its rector Bishop d'Hulst, he also incriminated the Biblical School. The editor of the *Civiltà cattolica* presented Father Lagrange, infatuated with historical criticism to the detriment of Catholic tradition, as the most dangerous promoter of the "broad school" in exegesis.

"I have kept silent long enough," reacted Father Lagrange, "to be allowed finally to defend myself against a new aggression that only dredges up old grievances." He recalled, then, the marks of confidence he had received from Pope Leo XIII and from Cardinal Rampolla. "I believe," he wrote to the master general, "that I should not allow it to be said that Pope Leo XIII was aiming at me in his letter to the French clergy. I think one should at least know how things were before Pope Pius X."

On the reopening of the Biblical School, Father Lagrange looked for but did not receive "a simple, kindly letter of the type he [the pope] writes so often." Father Lagrange did receive the encouragement of the master general, which he reproduced in the 1920 *Revue biblique*. The Biblical Institute, however, saw its plan for a foundation in Jerusalem approved by a letter from Pope Benedict XV, published in the *Acta apostolicae sedis*. Moreover, the encyclical *Spiritus Paraclitus* of December 15, 1920, drafted if not written by Father Fonck, no doubt stimulated the study of holy scripture, but certainly did not turn it in the direction advocated by the Biblical School. It denounced the positions of dangerous innovators suspected of not following the doctrinal line ordered by Pope Pius X. Father Lagrange was probably one of the exegetes at which it took aim. Some passages even seemed to revive the bygone quarrel between Father Delattre and Father Lagrange about *La méthode historique*.

At the start of the '20s, the future of the Biblical School of Jerusalem might have seemed threatened had Father Lagrange not been vigorously upheld by the unrestricted confidence of the new master general, Father Theissling.

The Defender

As soon as Father Lagrange was back in Jerusalem, haunting worries overtook him. He was comforted, however, by the resolute backing of the master general. Different from Father Cormier, whose reservations toward Father Lagrange's orientation were well known, Father Theissling made sure he was well informed so that he could effectively plead the cause of the school. As early as May 10, 1919, he had spoken about the school to the secretary of Extraordinary Church Affairs, Father Bonaventura Cerretti, and wrote to him the following day to confirm his arguments:

> It is of the utmost importance to avoid in the East dissension among religious orders. The prestige of the Catholic Church among the eastern churches would suffer greatly from this, since the Catholic Church alone gives the example of perfect unity.

It does not seem useful to us to hasten the destruction of a biblical school that was the only school in the Catholic world for a long time and that knew how to earn the esteem of scholarly circles in the Catholic world and elsewhere. If someone there has displeased the Holy Office, we are there ready to call him back.

We do not think it out of place, however, to note the respect Father Lagrange has gained by his more recent works where nothing worth condemning has been found, and on the other hand, to insist on the well-founded suspicion, which several competent and serious men have held, that during the campaign launched against him,... too many partisan and personal motives were involved.

Even though, in this case, the master general's approach was unavailing, his personal commitment on behalf of the school remained irrevocable. When the provincial of the Dominicans in Toulouse restored the *studium* of his province at St. Maximin, he requested the services of Father Lagrange. Master General Theissling responded that Father Lagrange's work in Jerusalem represented a higher value. "The Biblical School is...the work of your province, and I hope that it will always find sympathy and support among you. Let me go further. To those who might suspect or fear his teachings, I declare that I take upon myself complete responsibility for it. I have at the present time not the slightest doubt as to Father Lagrange's loyalty and orthodoxy, and I consider it of greatest interest for the church that his magnificent work should thrive and be supported, in a filial submission to authority."

In 1922, Master General Theissling showed his interest in the Biblical School by going to Jerusalem himself to make a canonical visitation to St. Stephen priory. It was the first time since the thirteenth century that a master general had visited the Holy Land. It was the first time since the foundation of St. Stephen priory in 1884 and the Biblical School in 1890 that the head of the order came in person to look into the intellectual activity and religious life of his sons. During Father Cormier's term, canonical visitations had only been made through delegates or by written reports. Announcing his intention on March 16, Master General Theissling visited in April, a short time after the accession of Cardinal Ratti to the Holy See. Cardinal Ratti was elected Pope on February 6. The master general's visitation directly concerned the relationship between the Biblical School and the newly elected Pope Pius XI. The presence of the newly elected pope, a well-known intellectual, aroused in Father Lagrange new hope for his biblical studies. "Pope Pius XI is a man who has a mind of his own and is not afraid to speak it. I am ready to obey his orders. His elevation is already an argument in favor of the church. The elevation of His Holiness Pope Pius XI seems to me to be a very happy one. What will he do for biblical studies? We do not know. It is comforting for us that he has always been a subscriber to the *Revue biblique*....Let us wait and see."

Master General Theissling arrived in Jerusalem thirteen days before Easter, on Tuesday, April 4, in the evening. "On arriving," said Father Lavergne, "he told us how happy he was to come and spend Holy Week in the Holy Land and his joy at visiting the Biblical School, 'one of the glories of the order.' After a long prayer at the burial site of St. Stephen, he told us that on leaving the Holy Father, the latter had expressed his hopes for the Biblical School."

The master general was very explicit. He opened his canonical visitation officially during Holy Week, at 2:30 p.m., Monday, April 10. After the usual short speech given to the whole community and after the lay brothers and the students had left the chapel room, the master general continued his meeting with the professors.

> You are not without knowing that a good many people—led by I know not what spirit—refuse to grant you the esteem to which you are entitled....Among them, some work more to supplant than to encourage

141

our Biblical School. During this canonical visitation, I shall try to find the reasons for this erroneous impression, and more particularly, by what means we can overcome this hostile prejudice. For our common solace, I can assure you that the Supreme Pontiff, Pope Pius XI, does not share the opinion of your opponents. During the private audience he granted me, he expressly assured me: "I have always had and still have as great a veneration for Father Lagrange as for his works. *Pro Patre Lagrange et studiis ejus, semper habui, quam semper retineo, magnam venerationem.*"

Master General Theissling then asked Father Lagrange to set out in a memorandum the reasons for the opposition shown toward the Biblical School. His response was a fourteen-page manuscript, simply written and full of crossed-out words. The memorandum was addressed to "My Most Reverend Father," and put confidentially into the master general's hands. None of the Jerusalem brotherhood, including Father Vincent, knew about it. Master General Theissling had an eleven-page copy of the manuscript typed out and authenticated it by appending a signature, "Written with his own hand, Father M. J. Lagrange, OP." Father Lagrange's words were direct:

You asked me to give you, in a few words, an account of the principal characteristics of opposition that the Jerusalem school has encountered from certain quarters. I feel very reluctant to do so, because, as your fatherhood knows well enough, such explanations will…seem a personal apology, and because it is always inappropriate for a religious to speak of himself at such length. I had rather say with today's antiphon: *Domine… responde pro me: quia nescio quid dicam inimicis meis.* But it is a duty for me to answer your request.

Let me first remind you of two points your two predecessors knew well. I never published anything that had not been examined by the censors whom they had appointed for me. I often had begged them to let me go back to my priestly occupations. They had known quite well that, if they took me away from biblical studies, they need not fear that I would make a scene or even the slightest delay. [In the end] they always told me to carry on my work here.

To be totally sincere and to put my conscience at peace, I must add that, if I obeyed all their formal orders, I did not always agree with them, especially the orders of Father Cormier, whose wishes I did not always follow in a positive way. It is obvious that he would have wished me to follow the opinions of the conservatives so as to incur no reproach. [Instead,] I simply left the domain of Old Testament studies, in which, let us be frank, I had brought upon myself the displeasure of Pope Pius X himself, but without consenting to campaign against the method and the propositions I had advocated. In doing so, I do not think I practiced the respectful or disrespectful silence of the Jansenists, for I always declared that I submitted *with all my heart* to whatever the Holy See might wish....It seemed legitimate to me not to anticipate his formal decisions, even in regard to opinions the Holy Father, Pope Pius X, was inclined to favor, because that method and those propositions, when examined under Pope Leo XIII, by the Holy Office, had not been condemned, and because Pope Leo XIII had shown me a favor later on that was no less explicit than Pope Pius X's apprehension.

That is at least how I formed my conscience. For, I say this before God, the reason why I gave such importance to the Holy Father's opinion was to be at peace with my conscience and, consequently, with God, as the pope is, on this earth, the representative of Our Lord Jesus Christ.

In this memorandum, Father Lagrange devoted ten pages historically documenting the attacks against him. He wrote about the first attack in 1898 concerning the Pentateuch, about Pope Leo XIII's plans in 1903 to settle the biblical question, and about the widespread public protest against *La méthode historique* during the first years of Pope Pius X's term. He told of the interdiction of the publication of the commentary on Genesis, of Father Fonck's maneuvers to establish an institute in Palestine, and of the disapproval of his works that appeared in the decree of the Consistorial Congress in 1912. Father Lagrange concluded with a declaration. "I declare, that since Pope Leo XIII's death, I have never gone further than the position that had the clear agreement of Pope Leo XIII and of Cardinal Rampolla."

In spite of the blame given in 1912, with the approval of Pope Pius X, the *Revue* had continued as it had been. Father Lagrange went back to Jerusalem in July 1913, with the agreement of the Holy Father, to take up his courses again. He had not been obliged to retract anything, nor to make statements of any kind in the *Revue biblique*.

In addition to Father Cormier, Father Lagrange mentioned his gratitude to Cardinals Mercier, Sevin, and de Cabrières, who were kind enough to stand up for him in Rome. "In disciplinary matters, one only has to take into account the degree of authority with which a minister of the church is invested. But once submission is given according to this supernatural principle, can one not regret that the Holy Father had less opportunity to consult those very learned prelates, rather than Cardinal Merry del Val and Cardinal de Laï, who wanted the public to see their total incompetence?...But I only want to consider my own faults that I submit to your leniency."

These words ended the first draft, signed and dated in Jerusalem on April 11, 1922. Immediately afterward, Father Lagrange added a postscript:

> One last word. I know the Holy See itself can adopt two different attitudes on some questions, and that after a question has been examined again more maturely, the faithful must hold to the new decision. But still, there has to be a decision, and I did not think that thousands of exegetical questions could be settled in a different way because a new pope had more conservative tendencies than his predecessor did. It seemed to me that, in good conscience, I only had to adhere unhesitatingly to official declarations, which I did, and to show total obedience to the general directions, which I did by forsaking the Old Testament and by conforming to the decision of the Biblical Commission for the New Testament, especially for the commentary on St. Luke.
>
> If one also objects to the need not to upset Catholic opinion, one would have to be blind not to see that in most parts of the world, those parts where people study it [the Bible], the vast majority of those specializing in holy scripture agree with the *Revue biblique*. This is true of the Society of Jesus, at least in England, France, and Belgium, not to speak of the Bollandists, its most learned body.
>
> All this said, I am awaiting from you, my Most Reverend Father, the words that will enlighten my conscience and govern it. I am equally expecting them from the Supreme Pontiff. *Nunc ergo (Petre) omnes nos in conspectu tuo adsumus audire quaecumque tibi praecepta sunt a Domino* (Acts 10:33).

In the end, the matter remained for the pope to decide. Master General Theissling, ending his visit at St. Stephen priory on Holy Saturday, April 15, concluded that, for the school to be rehabilitated, it would need to obtain the right to grant pontifical biblical degrees. "On behalf of the Biblical School, we must direct our efforts at obtaining the pope's authorization of a biblical license. This license would dispel at once the discredit wrongly heaped upon the school."

Once back in Rome, Master General Theissling was unable to get the immediate audience with the pope for which he had hoped. "The Holy Father has been so busy these last days that it has not yet been possible for me to approach him. But my audience will not be long in coming, and I shall most certainly let you know its results." The master general received word that Pope Pius XI would see him on June 28. Before the meeting, he prepared the Holy Father by sending him on June 23 "a confidential report...on the canonical visitation of St. Stephen priory in Jerusalem." The note which quoted several passages from Father Lagrange's memorandum, gave an exact description of the situation of the school and vigorously pled the cause of Father Lagrange but did not directly present any request to the pope. Master General Theissling was probably waiting for the Holy Father's reactions during the interview before soliciting permission for the school to confer pontifical degrees. (This solicitation is reproduced in full in appendix I.)

The day after the audience, the master general gave an account of it to the prior of St. Stephen priory.

> I have just seen the Holy Father and spoke to him about our Biblical School and Father Lagrange. You know what my wishes and hopes are on this point. The Holy Father received me with great kindness. He told me that he had carefully read the plan that I had sent him a few days before. He asserted his personal feelings of veneration for Father Lagrange and how much he admired his works. "But," said he, "it is not surprising that such work should arouse contradictions. It has

always been so. People pass and what is good in their works remains for the well-being of the church." He wholeheartedly blessed Father Lagrange, the community of St. Stephen school and the works they carry on there. It would, just now, be premature to expect more. The Holy Father told me that he needs time to examine everything, to be fully aware of the problems, and that he will do so in a spirit of perfect goodwill. For the time being, my dear Father, we have to be content with that and know how to wait, patiently and humbly, for the hour of Providence.

After so much hope, the result was meager. Marks of esteem and a show of good will cost nothing and commit nothing. The school must be satisfied with kind words; its future remained as precarious as ever. Father Lagrange returned tactfully to the charge. "Father Vosté told me, my Most Reverend Father, that you kindly intended to offer His Holiness some of my commentaries richly bound. I was very touched by this idea, and I cannot tell you how grateful I feel. Let me tell you once more that I want absolutely nothing for myself. For the school, it would be very beneficial if it could give the same degrees on the same conditions, not as the commission, but as the institute of the Jesuit Fathers does."

Finally, Father Lagrange, whose ill health no longer permitted him to continue as director of the school and who had handed its leadership over to Father Dhorme, resigned himself to receiving nothing. "I know your extreme benevolence attached a great importance to obtaining a word of satisfaction from the Holy Father. But I ask you not to insist. The Holy Father wants to wait, to inform himself. This is very justifiable. But he cannot find anything wrong with your granting me some rest."

Though, in 1923, Father Lagrange had been released from the management of the school and from the editorship of the *Revue*, which had been taken up by Father Dhorme, he was not yet free of his troubles.

Attack and Absolution

In 1919, Father Touzard, a Sulpician priest, a professor at the Catholic University in Paris, and a contributor to the *Revue biblique*, published a monumental, resolutely critical study of the Pentateuch that marked a new openness in biblical research. As it was, moreover, sponsored by the French Jesuits, it could not escape the attention of Father Lagrange. "The fathers of the Society of Jesus have resumed the forward march. It is true they have done so by having Father M. Touzard speak in their stead. His article "Moses and Joshua," in P. d'Alès's *Dicitionnaire d'apologétique*, is a considerable volume. If they [in Rome] allow it to pass, anybody will be permitted to treat the Pentateuch quite freely, at least with respect for the real tradition, which I have always professed. I would be curious to know how they [Rome] will take this exegesis at the commission. Is this what His Eminence the Cardinal President asks for?"

The answer was not long in coming. It came not from the Biblical Commission presided over by Cardinal Van Rossum but from the Holy Office, now ruled by Cardinal Merry del Val, whom Pope Benedict XV had positioned there in order to remove him from the Secretary of State. Asked "if the doctrine as to the Mosaic authenticity of the Pentateuch recently presented can be taught without danger," the Congregation of the Holy Office answered on April 21, 1920: "No." Its answer was published in a decree of April 23 and promulgated in the *Acta apostolicae sedis* of May 1. As had happened to so many exegetes under Pope Pius X, Father Touzard's scholarly career came to a halt: "the year 1920 marked the end of Father M. Touzard's scholarly activity." Five months after this scholarly Sulpician had been condemned, the encyclical *Spiritus Paraclitus* rigorously confirmed the doctrinal line upheld by the Holy Office.

The news broke in Paris on December 17, 1923, in an article appearing in the *Journal des débats*. A similar article appeared December 18, in *La croix*. "The last editions of the *Manuel biblique* have just been proscribed, condemned, and put on the Index by a decree of the Holy Office, given on December 12, confirmed by the pope on December 12, and made public on December 15." Father Henri Garriguet, superior general of St. Sulpice, as well as Father August Brassac, the first concerned, learned of the existence of the decree through the press, before getting any direct communication of it.

Emotion flowed from the pen of Father Albert Condamin, who on December 20 immediately wrote to one of his confreres at the Gregorian university:

> It would be difficult to understand how a book that did not come under any censorship under Pope Pius X, at the time of Modernism and of the vigorous reaction against it, should today, after sixteen years, be blacklisted by the Index, in the pontificate of Pope Pius XI, whereas one had hoped to meet with more encouragement for biblical studies from Roman authorities and fewer threats against exegetes....One would like to know, if it were possible, the part played by the integrists in these repressive measures and to what extent the Supreme Pontiff has been informed of all this. On the whole, we expect Pope Pius XI to give a favorable impulse, an encouragement for hard work where a good Catholic does not seek human glory or his personal interest, but only tries to put truth into the light and to contribute to the triumph of true religion. The documents of the Holy See, these last years, do not give us anything positive in this sense for biblical studies. On the contrary, we see, in the condemnation of Father M. Touzard, and in that of the Vigoroux-Brassac-Ducher textbook, an invitation to keep quiet and not to worry about the progress that should be made.

Father Condamin also appealed to the Jesuit Cardinal Ehrle, asking him to intervene. "I am certain that the Holy Father would listen to him if he told him that sincere and devoted sons wish they could work for the honor of the church without being paralyzed by continuous threats."

Even worse, and stranger, too, was that the promulgation of the decree against Father Brassac in the *Acta apostolicae sedis* of December 31 was accompanied by a violent indictment which Cardinal Merry del Val addressed to Father M. Garriguet on December 22:

> Numerous and serious defects have pervaded and vitiated the whole book, to the point that it would be absolutely impossible to correct it. Indeed, the author enumerates with a kind of indifference the arguments in favor of the traditional opinion, whereas he carefully sets out the critical arguments that support the new opinions without a word to point out their inanity and their weakness. On several occasions, the interpretations he offers go against the sense of the church. Without always adopting the opinions of the "broad school," which he presents with certain complicity, he nonetheless leans toward them. The least we can say is that he does not take the slightest notice of the decisions of the Biblical Commission. In short, he continuously goes against the orders of the magisterium, contradicting the tradition of the church. He flouts both the encyclicals of Pope Leo XIII and Pope Pius X, and the decrees of the Holy Office or of the Biblical Commission. Thus, no part of his work can escape reprobation.

News of the condemnation reached Jerusalem on the evening of December 26. Cardinal Tisserant sent it. Father Lagrange asked him to assure Father Brassac of his sympathy. It had probably also been forwarded to Father Louis Venard, as

Father Lagrange wrote to him on January 4, 1924. "You tell me about poor Father Brassac. I am very sorry for him. It is a plot against St. Sulpice, with whom others have associated themselves in the hope that thereafter it will be found necessary to strike at the principal culprit. Will the plan work? God knows. A long time ago, twenty-five years exactly, I resigned myself to everything, thinking it was a hard road but useful to the general good. [I was] always ready, in fact, to stop my work at the slightest order. As this order has not come till now, I keep on working as much as my greatly reduced strength allows."

It was absolutely certain that underlying the attack on Brassac was an attack on Lagrange. To defend the founder of the Biblical School, Professor Jacques Vosté, perhaps at the urging of Master General Theissling, prepared a "Note on the Works of Father Lagrange." He ended with these words:

> He has fought against Loisy, Reinach, Renan, and others. By his *Studies on Semitic Religions*, he has refuted the rationalistic science of comparative religions. By his *Studies on Jewish Messianism*, he has opposed unbelieving Israelites, adversaries of Jesus Christ. By his commentaries on the epistles to the Romans and the Galatians, he counters Protestant doctrines; and he has given us, through his works on the gospels, commentaries that replace and outdo anything produced by the Protestants. Why should we blame, in his later days, a man who has so well served his Mother and her holy faith....Why cast discredit on so many works which honor our Church and its scholarship?

Once the master general's letter had been communicated to Father Lagrange and to the other professors, anxiety pervaded the school. Father Dhorme alluded to this anxiety on January 31:

> The condemnation of Father Brassac's textbook has indeed greatly surprised us, for it is a very moderate

book. We have been warned, from different sides, that this could be a prelude to a campaign against our school, and it has equally been made clear that one of its leaders may be Father Fonck, of the Society of Jesus. We hope that the watchful attention of the authorities of the order will succeed in foiling ploys inspired by prejudice. We are sure that your Most Reverend Paternity, whose concern deeply moves us, will use this great moral and religious authority so that so much work, which has done the greatest honor to the order of St. Dominic and to Catholic scholarship, should not be lost.

The storm seemed to have veered away from the school. According to the master general, who answered on February 13, "I do not want to hold back any longer before giving you some news that will certainly be as valuable to you as it was to me. I have just learned, from a very reliable source, that the threat directed against Father Lagrange, which was all too real, can for now be considered dispelled. This does not mean that it may not turn up again; but, for the time being, the danger has been averted. Providence will help us again if need be and if we deserve it by our trust."

At the Biblical School, all breathed more freely. "The news you were kind enough to send us," wrote Father Dhorme on February 21, "brought me the greatest joy. I immediately imparted it to the person who was principally concerned and to the professors who know our anxiety. I cannot tell you how grateful we all are here, for the fatherly care with which you encourage and uphold our work, while it is still more or less threatened."

As for Father Lagrange, he remained in his usual frame of mind. "I am at once embarrassed at always giving you the bother of defending me and very moved that you should not be weary of doing me that good service with such a fatherly feeling. I thank God and your Fatherhood for the success of the steps you are taking. I dare say, I was not anxious for a single day because I feel in a disposition to obey in all things the Holy See and you, Most Reverend Father."

For once, the vigorous defense put up by the order against the foul insinuations had parried the thunderbolt without, however, disarming ill-willed accusers. The *Civiltà cattolica* of June 7 published an apology "for the recent condemnation of the *Manuel biblique*." It was known to have been written by Father Albert Vaccari, and it was said, in Rome, that the pope had asked for it in order to cut short the controversies. The author explained that Father Brassac went astray because he had followed the three principles of the so-called broad school, which had ruined the veracity of scripture. The principles concerned: the distinction between the substance of the facts or speeches and the secondary details, the distinction between a simple statement and a categorical assertion, and the distinction between the essentially religious aim and the narrative framework of the story. These principles imply the use of alleged literary genres, every one of which, even legend and myth, could be compatible with inspiration, as well as an appeal to the ruinous theory of historical appearances, as alien to history as scientific appearances are to science. The Holy Office had been of service to the authority of scripture by condemning a textbook "that affirmed the special theories of the *broad school* and the *new exegesis* of certain Catholics." What about names? The article did not mention any. If a frank reader required more knowledge of the subject of the new exegesis, an unobtrusive note sent him back to the comments of the encyclical *Spiritus Paraclitus* in the *Civiltà cattolica* of 1919. Only there would he find out about *La méthode historique* and about its author, Father Lagrange, who had fought for the new exegesis.

The Holy Office, too, remained as relentless as ever. Continuing its offensive against the suspect innovations, on May 5, it sent to religious superiors a circular on the study and teaching of the Bible. The instruction ordered that professors should not depart from the norms and orientations decreed by the Holy

See. Readers were referred to the *Providentissimus* of Pope Leo XIII, the *Pascendi* of Pope Pius X, the *Spiritus Paraclitus* of Pope Benedict XV, and also the decree *Lamentabili,* as well as the decisions of the Biblical Commission. It sought to join theology to criticism and pastoral exegesis to historical exegesis. It especially demanded that the control over teaching, the textbooks, and publications concerning the Bible be reinforced; the responsibility would rest with the superiors general. In July, the master general circulated the directives of the Holy Office. On November 9, Father Dhorme answered laconically, hinting that it was a waste of time: "The school uses no textbook; the students use the biblical text, the director does not state that the professors had departed from the norms decreed by the magisterium of the church."

During the aftermath of the Modernist crisis, suspicion continued to show its virulence until 1924. By 1925, in spite of a few sporadic skirmishes, a tacit armistice, probably encouraged by Pope Pius XI, put an end to open hostilities. The exegetes, however, had received no greater liberty to publish their critical research. For that, they had to wait until after the Second Word War, in the pontificate of Pope Pius XII. Even though the arrival of the Biblical Institute in Jerusalem in 1927 had not justified the apprehension Father Lagrange had kept rehearsing, the Biblical School's official situation, in the eyes of the church, remained shaky, until the pontificate of Pope John Paul II. The Biblical School was accredited to give the pontifical doctorate in biblical studies by a decree of the Congregation for Catholic Education, on June 29, 1983, fifty-six years after the accreditation of the Biblical Institute as a pontifical school.

The heroic patience shown by Father Lagrange and his disciples was at last bearing fruit. The church authorities, more obsessed by the Modernist danger than concerned for their own cultural backwardness, had been particularly late in acknowledging the service rendered their cause by the École biblique. By 1943, Pope Pius XII had affirmed the need to pay attention to the various literary genres present in the Bible in his encyclical *Divino afflante Spiritu*. This was the precise point made by Father Lagrange in his Toulouse lectures of 1903. The recognition came forty years after the proposal had originally been made. It came six years after Father Lagrange's death in 1938.

Chapter X

A ROMAN BENEDICTION

About 1925, when Father Lagrange had reached seventy years of age, he stepped away from the rigors of school administration and biblical research with relief. The future of the Biblical School now seemed assured. The team of disciples he had trained was ready to take over. All had become uncontested masters in their areas of study. All were in the prime of life. Father Jaussen, fifty-four, the dean of the Biblical School and a specialist in Arab ethnology, was the oldest. The youngest, Father Carrière, was forty-two and a professor of Hebrew. The archaeologist Father Vincent was fifty-three, the epigraphist Father Savignac was fifty-one, and the historian Father Abel was forty-seven. The expert in Assyrian culture, Father Dhorme, who assumed many of Father Lagrange's duties, was, at forty-four, the prior of St. Stephen, the director of the Biblical School, and the editor of the *Revue biblique*. Among the current students attending classes from 1923 to 1925, several Dominicans showed potential for the future. Some demonstrated leadership qualities, while others excelled in research and biblical studies. Fathers Lavergne, Braun, Tonneau, Arb, Duncker, Barrois, and Marmadji found places for themselves in the scholarly world almost immediately.

About the same time, Father Lagrange began to suffer from severe health problems in the form of disquieting fainting, progressing to slight heart attacks. These were often triggered by some emotional shock, the death of his sister Pauline in December 1924, for instance. He was forced to rest for long periods. At times like this others would think of a well-deserved retirement. Not Father Lagrange. He would consent to stop only if he were forced, and never completely interrupted his toil. He took advantage of his forced leisure to write his *Personal Reflections and Memoirs* for his brothers at St. Stephen. Written in March 1926, the *Memoirs* would not be published until 1966, forty years later

New Intellectual Projects

Since 1911, Father Lagrange had published commentaries or books on every one of the gospels: Mark in 1911, Luke in 1921, Matthew in 1923, and John in 1925. These were enormous volumes running from six hundred to seven hundred pages and more. This series was followed by a Greek synopsis of the gospels in 1926, then translated into French in 1927 with the collaboration of Father Lavergne. These works were not yet finished when Father Lagrange began thinking about devoting a historical apologia to Jesus Christ. He saw this work as a preparation for Christianity. The project was never realized, however. A portion of the work would appear in the *Introduction to the Study of the New Testament*. Different selections would be successively published in 1933 *(History of the Canon)*, in 1935 *(Textual Criticism)*, and in 1937 *(The Mysteries)*. Father Lagrange felt each work might be his last. He wrote to his sister on June 18, 1926, "I have often thought that after the *Commentary on St. John*, I would say *Nunc dimittis.*"

During the autumn of 1926, at Montpellier, when preaching at a retreat for the Dominican Sisters of Les Tourelles, whose intellectual orientation he appreciated and encouraged, Father Lagrange had a heart attack during the night of September 29. He was taken immediately to the hospital. In November, just as he was preparing to board for Jerusalem, a new attack returned him to St. Joseph Hospital. "He believed he was on the threshold of eternity," reported Father Vincent. It was "a crucifying" experience, Father Lagrange confided to Father Vincent in July 1927.

"He told me in a few words," said his confidant, "that, in the middle of last November, at St. Joseph Clinic in Marseilles, he had felt the stranglehold of death and the supernatural barrenness of a life eaten up by study. He had beseeched the holy Virgin to obtain mercy for him. After a few days of true agony, she had restored his inner peace. She inspired him to make a resolution to busy himself exclusively with making people know and love her divine Son, if he were only given a little more time and strength. If this work comes to fruition, it is 'the holy Virgin who will have done everything,' concluded my Master, enjoining me to pray to her with that intention."

After having spent several months in convalescence at Hyères, then at the Priory of St. Maximin, Father Lagrange was well enough to leave for Jerusalem on April 29. He arrived there on May 4. He had been away eleven months. During the summer, on St. Mary Magdalene Day, so as to keep his resolution of November, he decided to write "a kind of life of Jesus." After catching up on his correspondence, he settled down to work on the life on August 20. From then on, he kept worrying that he might die before the promised book was finished. In December 1927, a new health crisis compelled him to interrupt his work. No sooner had he recovered than he had devoted himself totally to the gospel of Jesus Christ, "imploring the holy Virgin to obtain for him the possibility of bringing the book to its term, considering that that would be the most salutary preparation for death." In fact, the foreword confirmed the confidences reported by Father Vincent. "While writing this essay," confessed Father Lagrange, "I never stopped imploring the help of the holy Virgin Mary. I beseech her to bless it."

"I'm far from being well enough to meet all my obligations," admitted Father Lagrange on January 19, 1928. "The worst is that I put the completion of *The Gospel of Jesus Christ* before anything else. I am writing it," he pointed out to the prioress of the Tourelles Sisters, "thinking of you and your nuns as a friendly audience." This was the book's purpose. "I write for simple souls," he explained in August 1927, "with no scientific pretension." The Dominican Sisters of Les Tourelles received repeated confidences as to the utility of the book. "Your community is, for me, the dreamed-of audience" (July 20, 1928). "I am even sure to be ill-treated by the specialists who will not find me scholarly enough. I must say that I count more upon the good souls who will be attracted by a book offering as impersonal a presentation of the gospel as possible, in the least sophisticated style" (January 7, 1929). Mr. Gabalda, his editor, however, would not hear of this catering to the masses. Father Lagrange would rather have had a popular edition of *The Gospel of Jesus Christ* "taken up by manual laborers, who begged…[him] to spare them the slightest display of erudition" than the deluxe edition, intended for bibliophiles, that his cousin Férier, a manufacturer in Lyons, would obtain for him.

Father Lagrange was worried. Would the public for which he intended to write understand him? "It seems to me that my book has quite a few luminous points, but as usual, and in spite of myself, it can only be for [intellectuals]; I cannot manage to reach the real general public" (May 10, 1928). On July 20, 1928, he wrote: "In spite of my intentions, I did not manage to extricate myself from scholasticism, and it will not be an enjoyable book for the general public." Father Lagrange equally reproached himself for the excessive haste with which he had written it: a book of 656 pages in six months. His taste for critical information and historical accuracy had prevailed over pious considerations and contributed to the scientific dryness of the style. "I would have liked it to have been above reproach as to information and criticism. There is so little pious reflection in it that I hardly dare say its aim is to let people get to know Our Lord Jesus Christ better." Would the book be approved by the Roman censorship? When, in October 1928, Father Lagrange had not yet received the printed proofs, he began to feel alarmed. According to Father Vincent, "He was persuaded that the delay must be due to some doctrinal difficulty or to an official intervention. His touching humility was not slow to discern the obvious motives justifying the blocking of the publication, if they did not even demand its total suppression, as they had done for the commentary on Genesis in 1905."

The master general's French assistant had done his best. "I have had his *Life of Jesus* examined by the censors who are both the most kindly disposed toward his work and most in favor at the Vatican. I have every reason to think that he will not only avoid getting into any trouble but that this magisterial book will get an approval from the Vatican, which will be like the seal of the church on all his earlier works." Not only did no difficulty arise, but the book obtained a success that none of Father Lagrange's other works had ever received. Three-thousand copies were sold in three months. In 1939, the print run increased to 26,000. The Roman benediction, for which he had waited so long, came at last on March 25, 1930, under the pen of Cardinal Pacelli.

Hostilities lingered. Near Christmas 1931, the superior of an Italian seminary, troubled at seeing the fondness of his seminarians for Father Lagrange's *Synopsis* and *The Gospel of Jesus Christ*, asked for instruction from the Congregation of Seminaries. Its secretary, the future Cardinal Ruffini, advised against giving them satisfaction: seminarians need piety more than learning. And Father Lagrange's work, especially in the case of *The Gospel of Jesus Christ*, was not of a kind to foster devotion!

Father Dhorme was elected prior of St. Stephen in 1919, and again in 1922. He was at the head of the priory from 1919 to 1925. From 1923, he was given the direction of the Biblical School and, consequently, of the *Revue*, on the advice of Father Lagrange. At the end of the academic year, 1930 to 1931, this fifty-year-old man, now at the head of the Biblical School for eight years, was preparing for his departure. He organized the teaching roster for 1931 to 1932, without including his name. He asked for permission not only to stay in France but also to leave the order. Father Lagrange was aware of none of this at the time. "We rejoice in advance," he had written on April 24, 1931, "in the very brilliant success Father Dhorme is sure to have in Louvain. I really wish the Academy of Inscriptions would recognize his merit as the best Semitist in France." During the summer when Father Lagrange had been informed that Father Dhorme would not come back to

Jerusalem, he was perfectly discreet, but his personal distress can easily be guessed. "Our work is in a very difficult situation. We need an almost miraculous help."

By September, Father Lagrange admitted his utter helplessness. "This misfortune is a deathblow for our poor school; it is the end, in confusion and shame. God grant us, on the contrary, that it may be a sign of salvation. But how can we hope for such a thing?" (September 12). "We are sorely struck. It would be the end if the Reverend Master General were to decide not to uphold us, but what a blow to public opinion!" (October 21). The direction Father Dhorme had imparted to the Biblical School was leading to the failure of the great design that had presided at its foundation. The theological goal of biblical studies and the spiritual climate in which they were to be steeped were not respected. Father Dhorme was causing the Biblical School to drift towards pure Orientalism, along the line of his personal choice. "After his book on Job (1926), which is a very fine work," Father Lagrange explained to the master general, "Father Dhorme told me quite clearly that he was giving up biblical studies....It became an axiom that the school and its *Revue* were dedicated to Orientalism, at least, in the opinion of some....Perhaps, after all, Father Dhorme's basic reason—it would be that of a high conscience, worthy of respect—is that, having no taste for the inspired books nor for archaeology, he no longer wants to be at the head of a biblical and archaeological school." The crisis might be a signal for salvation. "I believe," Father Lagrange again advised his superior, "that it would be good to give our course a violent change if we are to keep a biblical school here. Evidently—this is at least what I think—we should come back to serious biblical studies, without neglecting the special aim of Palestinian studies. We should go back right now to our original direction" (July 12). Father Lagrange returned to his point again. "One could rather say, with some reason, that we had, here, neglected the study of the Bible" (October 21).

Father Gillet, the master general, shared Father Lagrange's views. By his order dated November 6, he intended to remedy the situation of the school:

> The school must first come back to its tradition as a biblical school; that is, a school where the efforts of all are focused on the study of the holy scripture needs, more than any other, an atmosphere of true piety, if it is to live, to develop, and to spread its influence....We are sure that the sacrifices of the professors of the Biblical School have weighed heavily in the eyes of God, seeing the way St. Stephen priory has, for fifty years, overcome the different hardships, some of which, at times, seemed to shake it to its very foundations. Once again, a biblical school is a school like no other. If our colleagues elsewhere cannot live other than within the solid framework of a convent life, how much more so in a school like that of St. Stephen, where the study of holy scripture calls to piety, as much as piety invites professors and students to study.

On the other hand, the direction of the school had to be rethought. Father Lagrange had offered to take up service again at least for a short period. "Perhaps I could fill in some gaps while we wait [for the canonical visit of the master general in 1932]. I must judge the situation as very critical to put myself forward in such a way." A visitor, sent to the school in utmost urgency by the master general, had appointed Father Lagrange the regent of studies. The letters that Father Lagrange had then sent to Father Gillet are full of affability. The promptness of Father Lagrange's obedience never failed. "The Very Reverend Visitor put me in charge of the regency, just when I thought I could really have some rest. But I do not hesitate to abandon myself to your direction. Besides the supernatural motive of obedience, I am induced to do so because I am sure of your goodwill toward this work, which needs a speedy help, today as in the future." In the same way, he wrote to the Sisters at Les Tourelles. "I have had to take up responsibility for the school again, with one class a week. Father Vincent is in charge of the *Revue biblique*. Those events and the assignment I have been given have put an end to my wondering about the next work to undertake."

Father Lagrange, nonetheless, did not hesitate at confiding to the master general the feeling of disarray into which the crisis threw him. "Since the visitor nominated me as regent, I cannot sleep. I feel more than ever, and this is an understatement, a deep wish to have to see to nothing, and to take no responsibility, after having incurred so many to the detriment of my necessary inner peace. Certainly through my own fault, but after all, I wish I could avoid the same occasions and causes for agitation. If, consequently, you judge it right, while there is still some time left, to grant me the favor of that rest, I would be very grateful. If, however, you think it is not advisable, I submit myself beforehand to the will of God, which will be shown to me through you."

Surely, the crisis would be overcome. "We can hope that, according to that particular providential rule, which I have seen at work for over forty years, that every crisis that threatens to destroy our school has only consolidated it." On May 20, 1932, Father Lagrange wrote to the Sisters of Les Tourelles, "Only God can pull the school out of its fatal situation; we need an almost miraculous, divine assistance." In a series of letters he documented the hurt. The "catastrophe" (October 21) has left "a very painful scar" (February 2, 1932), "an incurable bruise" (June 15, 1932), a "cruel wound" not yet cured in January 1938.

The heartbreak was, to a large extent, linked to the disappointment that had caused it: "There remains an inconsolable grief: the situation of him whom I thought I had equipped to be a great champion of the church. Let us hope he will say nothing against the church; this is my conviction, grounded on the deep knowledge I have of his nature. After that, God can show his mercy: I earnestly ask you to pray for that intention." Another word gives us an inkling of not only how deeply felt the ordeal was but also of the spiritual perspective of redemption Father Lagrange found in it. "I was sent to Egypt to get some rest," he wrote on February 2, 1932, "and there I was ill. It was necessary to pay, even physically, for our misfortune." In June 1932, from Montpellier, where he was staying with the Sisters of Les Tourelles, Father Lagrange confessed his state of dejection to Father Vincent. "I am physically very well, but my intellectual morale has been shattered. The wound cannot be cured. I give myself totally up to Our Lord's Mercy."

The Last Echoes of Modernism

In 1931, Loisy had published his *Mémoires*. Reading them aroused Father Lagrange's indignation, less for the way he himself was treated than for the spite shown against Father Batiffol. "That poor friend is quite vilely treated by Loisy." Neither could he admit that Loisy's best friends, Monsignor Duchesne, Archbishop Mignot, and Father Bremond, who had remained faithful to the church, should be misrepresented as crypto-Modernists and shown as imposters. As to Loisy's religious drift, Father Lagrange saw it strongly confirmed by the *Mémoires*.

What was he to do? Keep silent or write "a fair book" against Loisy? Father Lagrange's collaborators at the Biblical School were against any answer. "The opinion of the young here is very hostile to it" (July 13). "Everybody tries to divert me from doing anything" (August 16). "Most of my friends are absolutely opposed to it" (September 25). "The young ones did not go through the crisis. They think it is over, that we should go forward without stirring up the past. I think, on the contrary, that we must liquidate the past before we can go forward, and that the deep cause of Modernism still exists: a certain dissatisfaction at the inadequacy of Catholic works that do not tackle certain difficulties." Yet, we should show how we differ from Loisy, "explain how our method was different from his," not to claim our orthodoxy at the cost of his, but to reestablish the truth and to do justice to the movement launched by Pope Leo XIII. The faithful servants of the church must no longer be mistaken for hidden or avowed Modernists.

As always, Father Lagrange turned to the master general, whom he asked for a directive as to the *Mémoires.* "I have read them. After much hesitation, I have begun to write an answer to that insolent *factum,* not to elaborate upon his personal grievances toward Father Duchesne, Father Batiffol, and others, but to show that he was rightly condemned and that his intervention has hampered the good progress of studies such as Pope Leo XIII had conceived them. If you think it is better to remain silent, I will stop immediately. If not, I will continue with your blessing: It would be a medium-sized book."

The master general approved the plan: "As the Most Reverend Father encourages me, I count on God's help." Father Dhorme's departure provided an additional justification. Would those opposed to the school not see there a proof that their suspicions were well founded? It was Father Lagrange's duty to throw a light on the reasons that had always opposed the Biblical School to the teachings of Loisy. "It is to enlighten public opinion about our past that I have decided, with the approval of Father General, to write a small volume of two-hundred pages on Loisy's *Mémoires....*It is not an answer to his attacks, which rather do me honor, but a setting straight of the record that seems to me necessary." Perhaps it could also contribute by shaking biblical studies out of the intellectual torpor in which they were foundering, stifled by Roman censorship: "No fervor, no desire to find an answer to the problems!" He deplored this attitude. "Every flame has been smothered with the blaze." He wrote to the rector of the Catholic Institute in Toulouse, "I have decided to publish a small volume about the *Mémoires,* intending to collaborate with the idea you have so clearly and so firmly expressed that it is time at last to resume our forward march."

The publication of the book, entitled by the editor *Loisy and Modernism,* was to occur at the same time as the Holy Office's condemnation of Loisy's *Mémoires* and their placement on the

Index, June 25, 1932. The *Documentation catholique* of July 30 would publish, in the same issue, the decree of the Holy Office and the review of Father Lagrange's book. For once, ecclesiastical authority had nothing to say against his *anti-Loisy* work, as he himself called it. "It does not have the same tone as Father Lebreton's review in *Études*, which I find rather indulgent," he noted to one of his correspondents. "Charity ought not to take the place of justice." The nuncio in Paris liked the work. "His Excellency Monsignor Maglione told me he had read every line of it with great satisfaction and had sent two copies to Rome through the bishop of Oran, one to Cardinal Pacelli, secretary, and the other to Cardinal Sbarreti, prefect for seminaries. He seemed to me quite sincere in this appreciation." Yet, when Father Lagrange returned to his research on Genesis, his work received no better reception.

Chapter XI

AUTUMN HARVEST

Father Lagrange's Jubilee

In 1935, the Dominican prior of St. Stephen organized a celebration for Father Lagrange's eightieth birthday on March 7. There was no crowd and no pomp. Nobody was invited, either from the order or from the religious communities of the Holy See, except for the married layman Jean Guitton and the Abbé, Thellier de Poncheville, the latter having come on a pilgrimage with a few priests who were his personal friends. The gathering around the stove in the common room, the only heated place in the priory, was as warm as it was simple. Jean Guitton presented the octogenarian with a volume on his works, *Cahiers de la nouvelle journée*, volume 28, for which he had written the conclusion. By 1946, this collection of essays was translated into English as *Père Lagrange and the Scriptures*. Contributors would include Cardinal Liénart, as well as scholars such as Father Joseph Chaine and Father Gustave Bardy. At his birthday celebration, Father Lagrange had spoken last. He thanked everyone with a few simple words: "I must say that I have always been very happy in the order." The next day, as regent of studies, he sang the High Mass of St. Thomas Aquinas in the presence of the entire school. At the age of eighty, the school's founder was still at the head of his field. Father Lagrange's birthday was not only to be an occasion for unanimous tribute but also for heartbreaking disruption.

The Tribute

December 24, 1933, had marked Father Lagrange's golden anniversary as a priest. The occasion had already been celebrated in Catholic publications by an article written by a former student, Professor Gonzaque Ryckmans of the University of Louvain. "Le Père Lagrange" had appeared in *La revue catholique des idées et des faits*, on December 22, 1933. In 1935, the articles paying tribute to Father Lagrange were not numerous. An article by Father Albert Dufourcq appeared in *La revue des deux mondes*, on March 1; another by Father Paul Archambault was published in *La vie catholique;* and instigated by Monsignor Tisserant, Father Ignino Giordani placed an article with the *Osservatore romano* on May 16. In June, an article by Father Joseph Bonsirven, SJ, appeared in *Recherches de science religieuse*. Finally, on July 6, an article by Father Guiseppe Ricciotti was carried in *L'avvenire d'Italia*.

Father Lagrange was aware of the esteem Father Bonsirven had shown him for over twenty-five years. Writing to Master General Gillet, he said,

> The article is frankly and honestly favorable. See page 357, in which the author says: "but he [Father Lagrange] was still supported by the favors of Pope Leo XIII....Then came the sate of siege justified by the fight against Modernism. The frontline fighter felt he was the object of the highest and most persevering suspicion....When the situation calmed, little by little, confidence was restored on almost every side...." The spirit of the article is certainly that those suspicions were not well founded, at least with regard to the doctrinal heart of the matter, and that the hostile measures had only been justified by the circumstances. What Father Bonsirven could not say is that those suspicions had been well founded and events had been systematically organized by the Society of Jesus, directed by father Luis Martin, so as to cause the

ruin of our Dominican school that would be replaced by the society....If the Fathers admit today...in their French biblical review, that the suspicions were excessive, they should now, in all fairness, make a show of restitution. But as nothing of the kind can be hoped for, they should at least find it right that the École be given the same status as the [Jesuit] Biblical Institute since the École served as a model for the institute in every dimension except for that spirit [of honest critical inquiry] which they [formerly] thought they had to correct and to which they now give due credit.

On the occasion of these anniversaries Lagrange wanted no collection of essays in his honor. Yet he did authorize *L'Oeuvre exégétique et historique du P. Lagrange* (*Cahiers de la Nouvelle Journée*, 28), for that book enabled people to know his thought, disseminated in so many books and articles. It is said he was particularly touched by the fine and courageous testimonial Cardinal Liénart gave him in his preface. The initiative, which came from Joseph Chaine, the exegete from Lyons, a former student at the School in 1919–1920, could not have been taken without Lagrange having been aware of it.

"Theoretically," he wrote to Jean Guitton on August 11, 1934, "I am not supposed to know anything. Between you and me, as I could not prevent this initiative, which may be risky, I thought it would be wiser, even necessary, for me to make sure that ideas are not attributed to me which are foreign to my thought. That would have spoiled everything and led to an imbroglio. I communicated to that good friend [Father Chaine] the idea you suggested in your last letter, that nothing would be more helpful to show the impression made upon intelligent circles, those of laypeople and, if possible, academics. It would be important to say that the work has done some good, has impressed well the minds wishing for criticism without giving up safety." Later, on August 21, he wrote: "I insist upon reading what is attributed to me, the summaries extracted from my ideas, but it will not be the same when you speak of the impression it will make. For that, I rely upon your delicate tact, which is so well combined with philosophical depth."

The printing was finished on February 22, and the volume arrived in Jerusalem on March 6. Father Lagrange immediately thanked Father Joseph Chaine: "Very dear and good friend. You will forgive me for not calling you 'Sir' after so many proofs of your friendship. Your volume, for it is really yours, arrived last night just as the community gathered to offer me their fraternal best wishes. It seemed to me as if you were there yourself among us offering me that precious token of friendship. I skimmed through it: Everything in it is perfect and said with such tact that it gives no handle to ill will. After having been so well treated by my friends, I fear that God might tighten the vise to hold me in humility. Yet, let us go on. *Laboremus!*"

At the general meeting of provincials gathered in Rome from September 29 to October 3, the Order of St. Dominic associated itself officially with the tribute given to the founder of the Biblical School. "The Biblical School, let us say it loudly," exclaimed Father Gillet in his opening speech, "is the jewel of the order. For centuries people will sing the praises of the school for all that its head, Father Lagrange, with his collaborators, did to defend the honor of the church in the field of exegesis during a troubled period in the history of the church." Less pompous, the words of the chapter were no less laudatory than Father Gillet's words toward Father Lagrange. "During his whole lifetime, he unrelentingly composed and published works that are praised throughout the world, admired by scholars, by unbelievers as much as by believers, books in which he has ruined the arguments and the objections of the opponents." A personal letter from the master general, dated October 2, completed the celebration of the order's gratitude toward Father Lagrange.

The celebration of Father Lagrange's eightieth year had been unanimous. At least no discordant voice was raised, and yet, the critical position of the Biblical School was far from being unanimously accepted or adhered to unreservedly. Was Father Lagrange wrong to dread the ill will of the École's opponents? "If my opinion has some value in exegesis," he wrote to Jean Guitton in August 1933, "it does not count. It is rather suspect in regard to its orthodoxy by...ecclesiastical opportunism." He deplored that Rome had considered it appropriate once again in 1934 to take up measures of repression against his history of the Patriarchs. "It is very difficult, nowadays, to publish studies of the Old Testament. The exegetes still have as little liberty [as in 1907]." Later, "We really have been comrades in arms," wrote Father Lagrange to his Jesuit friend Father Condamin, "stricken on the same day, you for your *Isaiah*, and I for my *Genesis*. You have been more persevering than I, hoping in *spem contra spem*. Without having the courage to imitate you, I admire your assiduity at giving reasons. It is all a matter of personalities. When God wills it, progress will come as the easiest thing in the world, as at the end of Pope Leo XIII's pontificate."

"Always the same weight of the official exegesis, we dare not say the party line represented by the Jesuits at the Biblical Institute in Rome, continues to rein in the progress of biblical studies." Father Lagrange, in April 1934, congratulated Monsignor Bruno de Solages, the rector of the Catholic Institute in Toulouse, on his zeal for studies among the clergy. Of the others he said, "They are certainly not progressing....No keenness, no wish to get to the bottom of the problems. Every flame has been smothered at the same time as the fire....We hear Cardinal Ehrle, SJ, has died. He was rather broad-minded. There remains Father Bea, the worthy successor to Father Fonck."

The future appeared as bleak as ever. Writing in 1935 to a Dominican prioress with whom he maintained a confidential correspondence, he said, "I hardly can share your hopes for the school. If we have made a dent, we did so by sacrificing, quite willingly, the Biblical School. We can no longer receive ecclesiastical students, and our [students] rarely gain admittance to [Roman] examinations. These are very dark times."

Heartbreaking Disruption

Two factors would free Father Lagrange to retire to France, far from Jerusalem. One was his health that, according to the doctors, required his departure. The other was political. His removal would be helpful to the school. It would bury the past.

Father Lagrange could perceive in himself signs of advancing age. "I already fight with difficulty against a lack of memory and a certain intellectual weakening. It is more and more urgent for me to retire so as to prepare for death," he wrote on May 12, 1934. Another sign worried him. On January 15, 1935, he confided: "However cheerful I pretend to be, it is hard for me to fight against senile bitterness. Moreover," he added, "one point is quite clear. People often speak of the *theses* that have compromised the Biblical School, of the necessity of forgetting the past, and so on. Well, if we wonder of what the past consists, I must recognize that these reproaches are only directed against me. [They affected neither Vincent, nor Abel, nor Jaussen, nor Savignac.] Dhorme himself is more of a conservative than I am. So, the best way of showing that the past is really past would be to let me sink into oblivion, which the authorities are already willing to grant me."

When, in May 1935, he sent the program of courses for the school year 1935 to 1936 to the master general, his name could no longer be found on the list. He explained: "I no longer feel the strength to put myself down to teach a course, hoping you will be kind enough to excuse me because of my age. In this, however, as in everything else, I remain perfectly submitted to what you will decide. It is the same for my regency and my assignment. On those two points, I only ask you, my Most Reverend Father, not to act out of kindness toward me, according to the thought you expressed at Aix, because you do not want to look as if you disowned me. For if my distance can, in the slightest way, be useful to the École, I will accept it, not only without any sadness, but with joy, feeling besides the necessity to prepare for death in meditation and peace." To show his goodwill, Father Lagrange had agreed to give a few special lectures. "This, moreover, does not change anything about what I have just told you about my personal situation, which is not of much use here, if it is not downright unhelpful."

Illness was to put an end to hesitation. After Father Lagrange's serious bout with jaundice, the doctor at the French hospital reported on July 22 that his health "needed great attention," that "the Palestinian climate is really not advisable," and that the Father "ought to leave Jerusalem as soon as possible and go back to France." Five days later, Father Lagrange sent the chief medical consultant's certificate to the master general.

> I waited a few days before sending you this appraisal by the very competent doctor who has been looking after me for almost two months and who knows about my former illnesses. I feared to give too much importance to my own health. After having thought it over carefully, I think it is my duty to let you know everything, insisting that this consideration about my health should only count after all the others in the decision you will think you must make. I realize very well that, wherever I am, I can only be a boarder. I only add that the provincials of Toulouse have always declared that they would gladly accept me, so that I could prepare for everlasting life where I had prepared for Dominican life. I have spoken to absolutely nobody about this step so as to let you have total freedom in your decision.

When a second medical visit, asked for by the master general, had confirmed in September the recommendation given in July, Father Lagrange received a letter dated October 2, from Father Gillet, giving him his *Exeat.*

> If you send me with some regret the doctor's view declaring it was dangerous for your health to remain in Jerusalem, you know it is not without some sadness that I have accepted it. But the consultation I asked you to

have leaves no room for any doubt, and it is with the certainty that you and I have done whatever was necessary to obey the designs of Providence that I have signed the assignment that sends you back to your dear home province.

I do not want you to leave the school of which you were the founder and the soul and that will continue to live with the spirit you gave it, without thanking you, in my name and in the name of the order, for the glory you shed on it and for the services you rendered to the holy church.

Some time ago, I wrote that the Biblical School was the *jewel of the order.* I am pleased to repeat it now, as the provincial fathers, gathered here for the general chapter meeting, are preparing to take advantage of the occasion of your eightieth birthday to show a lively expression of their admiration and veneration.

When he had received his new assignment, Father Lagrange left Jerusalem very discreetly on October 6. He sailed on the *Champollion* with a student of the school who was going to Rome for an examination. "How deeply he must have suffered!" noted his companion. "But he never uttered a groan or a regret." After having landed in Marseilles on the morning of October 12, Father Lagrange arrived at the Priory of St. Maximin on that same evening. From there he answered the master general on October 21.

My Most Reverend Father,
    If I did not answer sooner the letter you sent me [October 2], it is not through ingratitude but because I knew not how to express my embarrassment at so much kindness. I am still incapable of doing so. Being, however, very sincerely and simply aware of not having deserved your kind words, I cannot tell you even that I shall try and do better, as my career is over. Yet, I must

tell you that the change of air, the fact of being free from cares have been very beneficial, and that I find myself once more in the state that was mine before that crisis, except for the weakening of my memory.

Moreover, my main concern must now be to prepare to appear before God.

Please accept, my Most Reverend Father, my total and deepest gratitude for what I dare consider the tokens of affection you have lavished upon me.

I am, most respectfully and obediently,

Your very humble,
Father M. J. Lagrange, OP

Father Lagrange's restraint masked the pain brought by this wrenching change. He kept it secret except from a few intimate friends. He wrote to Jean Guitton on December 15, 1935. "You surely understood how deep my sorrow was on leaving Jerusalem and my dear confrere, Father Vincent. After having shared so much over forty years!" He wrote to Father Robert Devreesse on January 3, 1936. "This change has restored my health...for a time, but how cruel it was to leave my faithful collaborators, particularly Père Vincent." The knife was only turned in the wound when, in July 1936, it became possible for him to return to Jerusalem. He wrote to Father Pierre Benoît on July 19, 1936, relating his most recent news. "I received communication from the master general adding that he wished me to choose if I wanted to return or to stay here. I immediately answered the mediator that I could not decide for myself, but if the master general expressed his own wish, I would immediately conform to it. I am too old to have a will of my own." Ready to obey as quickly as a young novice, Father Lagrange could not hide the health reasons that were an impediment to this return. As for the master general, it could not escape him that the reports were well founded. Father Lagrange would stay at St. Maximin. As the thought of death became more insistent, his nostalgia for

Jerusalem became more tormenting. Father Lagrange depicted his situation for Father Pierre Benoît, in January 1938. "Every now and then, in my sleep, I dream that I am taking a ship for Palestine. Usually, the weather is stormy, an image of your situation. But is not the whole world hanging over rocks, held only by a thin thread?" Jerusalem was constantly on his mind. He wrote to Father Denis Buzy, January 5, 1938, "By day or night, I often think, even in my dreams, of going back so that I could die in Jerusalem." On the same day, he wrote to Father Louis Marie Dewailly, "How much I wish I could go back and die there!"

At St. Maximin

In 1923, the province of Toulouse, which had just opened its house of studies at St. Maximin, had already tried to promote Father Lagrange's return. The reasons put forward by the provincial to the master general were not only intellectual. "The Most Reverend Father Prior rejoices over the good influence Father Lagrange would have on the community on all points, especially on religious life, according to the opinion of the novice master." When his request was rejected, the provincial expressed "a very painful disappointment." The first answer, a positive one, "brought us the invaluable advantage of having at St. Maximin such a distinguished and eminent religious for the formation of our students in respect to holy scripture and of regular life. It is the answer to a very detrimental situation." The novice master insisted in the same way. Our young students "would have constantly before their eyes a living and thought-provoking example of the practical love of our life, of study, and of regular observance."

In 1935, both the regent of studies and the provincial emphasized for the master general the benefits brought by the presence of Father Lagrange, not only intellectually but, even more, religiously. Father Claverie wrote to Father Gillet on December 15, 1935: "Reverend Father Lagrange does not find there the material facilities he had in Jerusalem. He says nothing about it, but we have tried to remedy it. Physically, he is well and keeps to his diet. Morally, he remains as nimble-minded as ever, keeping pace with the activity of the young in their work and in their brotherly joy. We are the ones who benefit most especially from the example of his virtue and of the qualities of his mind and heart."

In 1901, the order had awarded the degree of master of sacred theology to Father Lagrange. The master general himself had wanted to confer it in Rome on September 19, but in order to enjoy the rights and privileges linked to the master degree, Father Lagrange had to be acknowledged as a master in his own province. As long as he had been assigned to Jerusalem, the question had never arisen in Toulouse. On the provincial's initiative, the provincial council, in December 1935, then the provincial chapter in July 1936 asked that the master degree be confirmed, so that Father Lagrange could become a legal member of the councils and chapters of the province. The provincial chapter phrased their request in particularly laudatory terms:

We ask that the Most Reverend Father Lagrange be acknowledged as a master of theology in this province where he is already wanted and accepted, he whose praise echoes not only in our order but throughout the church. It would be futile and useless to assess his merit, his totally religious life, his vigorous and persevering work, or his astounding knowledge, or to enumerate the numerous books and articles he devoted to the gospels and to St. Paul for more than forty years. Nowadays, he shines like a bright light approved not only by Christians but also by unbelievers who admire him. With joy and gratitude the province of Toulouse, feeling rightly proud of having such a son, asks that he be ranked among the council fathers of the province.

Even though he managed to allay suspicion, Father Lagrange felt painfully diminished and in his decline. He confided to some intimate friends, writing on August 1, 1936, "They say I enjoy a blooming health, perhaps because I try not to moan too much and to keep on acting right to the end, but, in fact, I have to save my strength for what is strictly necessary....I make no more big plans, but I live from day to day. If only I applied that time to get ready to stand before God!" On October 4, 1936, he commented, "I am still at St. Maximin, exiled far from Father Vincent and my health is not getting much better. I go from one snag to another, but it is due to my age. I try not to grumble too much, if I can only be of some use to our young ones who are so studious"

In Jerusalem, Father Lagrange had probably forgotten how cold it could be at St. Maximin with the fearful lack of comfort in the priory. There was no central heating in the fourteenth-century Gothic building. The first winter was almost fatal to him. The provincial explained to the master general on January 21, 1936: "He got the flu and so badly that we thought he was going to leave us for a better world. But he got over the crisis, and he is getting better and better. He is beginning to get up, and the doctor has fully reassured us." In September 1936, Father Lagrange was unwell again. "I have again wasted about a fortnight with eight days in bed! It was in bed that I received His Eminence Cardinal Tisserant, who was kind enough to visit me," he wrote on October 11, 1936.

Sent to Cannes for his convalescence after the winter of 1935 to 1936, he wrote to his friend Father Albert Condamin on February 27, 1936. "I am no better in France than in Jerusalem. Studies are over!" To the hindrances due to his poor health were added those caused by the lack of intellectual means. The library was skeletal, lacking even the basic tools and not receiving any scholarly publications. The house was not devoted to study, at least not according to the strict manner of St. Stephen's. "Only in Jerusalem can one spend all one's time at work," he sighed. "Even without any students, the place would still be a *scriptorium* for *scriptores,* and that is what is needed, serious work, a recognized competence, as high a level and surer methods than those of the enemies of our faith. By that, the reputation of the school is made;

the order had better uphold it," he wrote to Father Pierre Benoît on January 7, 1937. He was haunted by the fear of letting himself sink into the bitterness of senility.

Yet, Father Lagrange had a new lease on life through contacts with the outside world. At Montpellier, where he retreated in March and December 1936, in September 1937 and again in February 1938, he was received by the Sisters of Ste. Marie des Tourelles. There his interest was revived in academic circles, and he contributed to the creation of the apostolic antenna for St. Maximin priory. A round of lectures on François Mauriac's *Life of Jesus* gave him the opportunity to speak at Aix-en-Provence, at Lyons, and at Marseilles. He reportedly addressed "a very interesting group of Catholic academics." Cardinal Pacelli even wished that Father Lagrange would consult on a revision of the *Life of Jesus.* "I have received no communication from the author, and I would be greatly surprised if he were to consult me. In an interview in *Les nouvelles litteraires* he even said he *leaned* on my authority. Of course, I did not quote those words, and had I known that he suffers from cancer of tuberculosis of the throat before beginning this campaign, I would probably not have started it. This cruel illness explains well enough his pessimism!" (June 1, 1936). Father Lagrange spoke in public at Toulouse in December 1936, at Aix during the spring of 1937. In the summer of that year, from August 25 to September 1, he was invited by layman Marcel Légaut at Chadefaud for "a spiritual holiday gathering" of Catholic academics. He gave them six lectures in the form of spiritual meditations. Among the audience was Father d'Ouince, the new editor of *Études.* Stemming from his activity as a lecturer came several publications: "François Mauriac's *Life of Jesus,*" "The Historical Realism of the Gospel according to St. John," "The Pythagorean Legends and the Gospel," and "Realism and Symbolism in Dante." These articles were published in the *Revue biblique* in the 1936 to 1937 volumes. "The Reading of the Bible and the Dominican Soul" was published in a 1936 issue of *La vie dominicaine.*

New Intellectual Plans

In May 1936, the red hat conferred on Eugene Tisserant, an alumnus of École biblique and a faithful friend of Father Lagrange, promised a slight improvement for biblical research. Cardinal Tisserant became a member of the Biblical Commission in June. "A piece of good luck has come to St. Stephen's," the French assistant remarked to the master general, "the conferring of the office of cardinal on one of its former students, one who has remained deeply attached to it. When Monsignor Tisserant answered the master general's letter, he did not conceal what he owes to Father Lagrange, whom he continues to venerate."

In 1936, several Catholic intellectuals, preoccupied with the need to unshackle research, had the idea of presenting the Roman authorities with a memorandum on the necessity of having in Catholic exegesis an enlightened and honest biblical criticism. That memorandum, written by Jean Guitton, "Remarks on the Situation of Catholic Scholars in France in Regard to Biblical Studies," October 1936, was only made public in 1987, in *Le Christ de ma vie, dialogue avec J. Doré*. Could the initiative coming from France overcome Roman inertia at a moment when, as Monsignor Tisserant admitted to Father Lagrange, "The Holy Father had no wish to deal especially with the biblical question"? The decrees issued by the Biblical Commission in the days of Pope Pius X would continue to hold sway and to weigh upon the conscience of Catholic exegetes for a while longer.

After his book on Orphism was published in August 1937, Father Lagrange had to face a choice. Should he go on with his research on the mystery religions, addressing only an initiated public passionately interested in the history of Christian origins? Or should he answer the questions of numerous Catholics troubled by the confrontation of scientific data and the Bible as to the origins of the cosmos and of man? Father Lagrange felt more than ever the need to tackle head-on the vital question of the primeval religious history recorded in Genesis, chapters 1 to 11. He would submit to the master general's decision.

The first solution would be not to do anything, except perhaps to write some small article or to give a short lecture. That does not appeal much to me, because I am presumptuous enough, perhaps somewhat recklessly, to believe that I can still work. Since Our Lord has left me some strength, it would be proper, I think, to apply it to his service. But I shall keep to your advice, if you judge that it would be better for me to prepare for death without undertaking anything.

Indeed, I am not so blind as to dare launch myself on a new track. I have had two subjects in the works for a long time now, and it is on the choice of one of them that I appeal for your decision.

I have completely written out a commentary on Genesis. Father Cormier approved it on the favorable advice of two censors. The printing had begun but was interrupted by order of the Holy See. I need not say that the new writing would be reshaped, but I could not do it in the manner of Father Bea, who deceived the public by an ambiguity. Wellhausen is in decline, and I have always vigorously fought him. But the documentary theory, far from losing ground, is more radical than ever. The decree of the Biblical Commission does not prejudge everything, since it admits the role of secretaries [in the composition of the Pentateuch], and that the facts recounted in Genesis occurred long before Moses. The capital point is the primitive history. The need for an explanation is very intense, insistent, irrepressible, among the best Catholics. It is amazing to see to what extent the teachers' world, which is not totally absorbed by social questions, is preoccupied by it. When the Jesuit Fathers Koppel, [Teilhard] de

Chardin, and others date humanity back to at least 100,000 years ago, it is on this point that teachers as Catholics ask for some light. Taking into consideration the general need, there is no doubt that this is the matter to be addressed. But the question is to know whether the Roman authorities would give a blunt refusal to this study. I don't think the opposition would come from the Biblical Commission. Could you supply information on this?

If the obstacle were insuperable, I would fall back on a work generalizing my articles on the mysteries of Eleusis of Attis, to which I have just added Orphism. It would be necessary to put these in order and to complete them. There would be some interest among the learned.

As usual, Father Lagrange left the decision to his superior, remaining indifferent, as he liked to say, not because he had no personal preference, but because he would accept the solution he was offered with the same goodwill.

Commentary on Genesis

A speedy answer was not forthcoming from Rome. The Dominican master general, Father Gillet, left on September 24 for a visit to the priories in the Far East. In his absence, the responsibility for making such decisions was to fall to the rather timorous vicar general. After having discussed the matter with the master general and his counselors, "We concluded," related the vicar general, "that Father Lagrange would be asked to do the work of revision he had mentioned without knowledge of when the appropriate time would come for its publication. The master general did not seem to think that a quick publication would be possible." Cardinal Tisserant, privately consulted, "fully shared our opinion, adding that the difficulty would certainly not come from the Biblical Commission, as he now was part of it, along with Cardinal Mercati. When I told him it would perhaps be necessary to wait for a long time before we could go to print, he reproached me for being so pessimistic, but he could not tell me that at the present moment there would be no difficulties." Roman decision makers, such as the Holy Office and the Congregation for Studies, not to mention a few fiercely aggressive watchdog organizations with no official mandate that vociferously spoke their minds as finicky guardians of orthodoxy, were still keeping their eyes open for problems.

In the answer from Rome, Father Lagrange saw a positive encouragement to take up again the critical research begun thirty years before. On October 15, he answered the vicar general: "I must really thank you for the letter of October 4, which authorizes me and even invites me to receive Genesis [as my work assignment]...without changing the spirit of the first commentary, as you foresee some difficulties for the publication. My conscience is greatly relieved, for it seems to me that you have no theoretical objection, or else you would not have asked that this work be done by an old man who must, more than ever, undertake nothing but for God. Consequently, I set myself to work with all my heart, leaving the result of it in the hands of God."

Before going back to Jerusalem, Father Hugues Vincent, now the editor of the *Revue biblique*, came to meet his friend at St. Maximin. "He is working actively to bring his commentary on Genesis up to date. His constant and tireless ardor for work, his love of souls, his supernatural spirit, and his wonderful serenity are, more than ever for me, the most effective lesson and the most rousing example. I will leave for Jerusalem on Tuesday morning [November 2] well restocked with courage, religious spirit, and goodwill.

Father Lagrange's work on Genesis had been shelved since 1907. To bring it up to date, he would have to review his critical text, his translations, and his annotation. Father Vincent had taken upon himself to send him, from Jerusalem, the new archaeological and historical documentation that had piled up over a thirty-year period. "This revision is in quick progress," noted

Father Vincent in November. "The laborious work in common was progressing rapidly," he remarked again in 1938. "We are working together thanks to a weekly exchange of letters. This allows a very close collaboration." As for Father Lagrange, he had very few illusions about the fate of his work. "This project on Genesis," he wrote to a sister of Tourelles on January 19, 1938, "has for the time being, no chance to succeed and should be kept secret." In late February 1938, however, the beginning of the manuscript, "Primitive History, chapters I to XI," was given to the Dominican Sisters des Tourelles to type in triplicate. Death soon interrupted the work, however, and only a preliminary study was published as an article. "The Mosaic Authenticity of Genesis and the Theory of Documents" appeared in the *Revue biblique* in April 1938, a month after Father Lagrange had departed life.

The Article on the Patriarchs

Updating the Genesis commentary was a long-term project. In 1907, to prepare public opinion, Father Lagrange had written an article on the Patriarchs that he thought especially important, but which the Roman censorship considered too provocative. "I have not written anything more seriously apologetic on the Old Testament," Father Lagrange commented.

By early 1938, Father Lagrange had hoped to publish the article he had written in 1907, and that had been refused publication ten years before in 1928. He wanted to insert the article, provided that it was not censored, in the January 1938 issue of the *Revue biblique*. For reasons of opportuneness detailed by the vicar general, the censors were more hostile to its publication than ever. First of all, as the vicar general explained to Father Lagrange, the subject was too delicate: "one of those which lays itself open to criticism." If the article were published, he warned: "Then our opponents, who have never let up for thirty years, might find there an opportunity to launch a new attack against the *Revue biblique*, or against the school of Jerusalem…[they] even might find there an argument to place a president hostile to the St. Stephen name at the head of the Biblical Commission." At last: "Time has worked and is still working for us. Should we risk setting this work back through our impatience?"

These were questionable arguments that Father Lagrange did not hesitate to contest. Let time work for us? "May I tell you that it works rather for routine. But, finally, this sentence supposes that times have changed and, consequently, that one can say today what was inopportune yesterday. The worst is that he seems to think that opportuneness is still against us." What of the future chairman of the Biblical Commission? "He will be such an important person that one of Father Lagrange's pranks could have no influence whatsoever on the choice." Too delicate a question? "In itself, the article is apologetic. I have often set forth in the *Revue biblique* the principle on which it stands: to defend a position, which, otherwise, would not be defensible."

In response to the vicar general's words, Father Lagrange wrote, "I can correct the text, take into account new observations, as much as you like. To replace the article would mean a month's work, and at the age of eighty-three, I already have a lot to do as I teach two classes a week!" But since from Rome, Father Lagrange received nothing but the order to wait, toward the end of December 1937, he decided to give up his article for the time being. During this time he bore in mind that Cardinal Tisserant, behind whom the vicar general was hiding, had not had the opportunity to study the corrections he had added to mitigate the text that had first been set up in type. The publication of his work on Genesis would not be introduced by the study on the Patriarchs but by the article on the theory of documents.

Father Dhorme Reviewed

"I have just read Dhorme's book, *L'évolution religieuse d'Israël*," wrote Father Lagrange to the vicar general on November 20, 1937, "and I have begun a long review that will be more to the point [than the Patriarchs' article]...but that article still has its importance, and Dhorme has not touched the main point." The major review, dated November 21, printed December 20, was intended for the *Revue biblique* of January 1938, instead of the article on the Patriarchs. In its first print version, the article began with a courageous declaration, crossed out later to blunt its edge: "Édouard Dhorme is not unknown to the readers of this review in which he has published so many articles that have done us so much honor. This makes it more difficult for us to speak here of his latest work." Afterward came ten pages in small print in which Father Lagrange discussed the evolution Dhorme thought he had found in biblical history.

From the Roman point of view, to treat the work of Dhorme, even to criticize him in a Dominican review, seemed unthinkable. At the same time, the publications of the French Dominicans had been causing serious trouble. Their weekly newspaper *Sept* had been forced to cease publication on August 27, for having taken favorable positions in regard to the leftist Popular Front government in France. *Sept* had also come out in favor of the Republican government in Spain, even though it was persecuting the church during the Spanish Civil War. "The cessation of *Sept* has caused a great disappointment in this milieu," noted Father Lagrange on September 5. "I remain very reserved." *La vie intellectuelle* had just published a thunderous editorial on September 10 entitled "The Church Body of Sin." The article was followed by another by Father Henri Guillemin, "Through Our Fault," that had greatly irritated Pope Pius XI and had brought the review a severe warning from the master of the Sacred Palace in the *Osservatore romano*. Under these circumstances, the vicar general thought it was better to keep silent about Dhorme. "Once more the wise are going to pay for the stupidity of the fools," he explained to Father Lagrange, "but this is a law of our poor fallen nature."

The January issue of the *Revue biblique* had progressed to the final page design when a telegram from the vicar general ordered the editor to "withdraw, for the time being," Father Lagrange's article. The editor, Father Vincent, Father Lagrange's longtime friend, handed over his resignation on the spot. Father de Vaux, who finished the editing of the January issue, replaced him without warning. Father Lagrange, offended at a refusal prior to any examination of the basic content of the article, asked the master of the Sacred Palace to examine the rejected text himself. The professors in Jerusalem concluded that it was becoming more difficult than ever to examine the questions that were, in fact, the most urgent ones. "It is no longer possible to find anybody willing to risk publishing a serious article on the Old Testament," noted one of the administrators at the Biblical School.

The censors rejected the famous scholar until his last days. He never deviated, however, from his religious submission. Even when he resorted to the master of the Sacred Palace to ask for a new examination of his review of Dhorme's article, "It is not at my age," he declared, "that I wish to retract the firm resolutions I took to practice the most total and filial obedience." As a conclusion to this painful incident, Father Vincent related that he received from Father Lagrange "a letter, as firm and supernatural as affectionate, renewing his instructions that I should maintain an attitude of rectitude and absolute sincerity in my judgments, of unfailing energy in the fulfillment of the task obedience had allotted to me, and above all, of a deep religious spirit and trusting abandonment to Providence. It was a real spiritual testament and the example of his own life that reinforced its ability to penetrate my heart."

The Death of Père Lagrange

During the last week of February 1938, the bishop invited Father Lagrange to Montpellier. There, he gave a lecture at the major seminary, and a few talks to the Sisters of Tourelles, to groups of educated Christians, and to male and female students. He had discussed Loisy's latest book, *Histoire et mythe à propos de*

Jésus Christ, with Jean Guitton, who had sent copies to him previously. He had even gone with a few friends to admire the pre-Romanesque abbey church of St.-Guilhem-le-Desert. Back at St. Maximin on the afternoon of March 1, he received the next day, Ash Wednesday, a visit by his disciple Father François Marie Braun. On Thursday, March 3, in a letter to Father Vincent, he stated that the week at Montpellier had "shaken his intellectual torpor."

On Friday, March 4, he gave the Dominican students his course on the passion narrative in St. John and the synoptics. On Saturday, March 5, he corrected the proofs of his article on the "Mosaic Authenticity of Genesis" for the April issue of the *Revue biblique*.

On Tuesday, March 8, his eyesight blurred, his breathing became difficult. He had to give up all work. The doctor diagnosed a congestion of the lungs, which quickly grew worse. Father Lagrange, told how serious his state was, thanked the doctor, and received extreme unction: "I give myself up to God." These were his last cognitive words. During the night those who were sitting by his bedside said they heard him whisper, "Jerusalem, Jerusalem...."

Father Lagrange passed away peacefully, on the morning of Thursday, March 10, 1938. He was surrounded by his brethren, who sang the *Salve Regina*, according to the Dominican custom. On Saturday, March 12, the Dominican community laid his mortal remains to rest in the center of the convent cemetery, inside the garden enclosure.

Since November 12, 1967, Father Lagrange's ashes, exhumed from St. Maximin, have been buried in Jerusalem, in the Basilica of St. Stephen, at the foot of the altar, under the great stone slab brought from St. Maximin. The inscription recalls what a tireless defender of the Word of God the founder of the Biblical School truly was. There where he prayed so regularly with his brothers, the prayers of his disciples continue to surround him. The bubbling spring created by God continues to flow silently on.

"I feel great sorrow at not seeing approved so many efforts which were, I thought, well intentioned. I hope that future theologians will acknowledge that I sacrificed nothing essential, that I defended this essential *unguibus et rostro*, and that it will be necessary, like it or not, to practice a serious literary and historical criticism." These words, dated December 1925, remained permanently true throughout Father Lagrange's life. Cardinal Tisserant was appointed president of the Biblical Commission in July 1938, four months to the day after Father Lagrange's death. Father Jacques Vosté, a Dominican and another of Father Lagrange's disciples, was nominated secretary to the commission in May 1939. The path of liberty had been opened for Catholic biblical scholarship.

Chapter XII

CONCLUSION

Inspired by the Parisian model created by Victor Duruy, Father Lagrange had founded the Practical School of Biblical Studies in Jerusalem. By the disciples he formed, he had become the master of the school. By the scholarly impulse he transmitted, he had, in all truth, created a new school of thought. On the occasion of the school's fiftieth anniversary, a former student, Monsignor Bruno de Solages, compared the school at Jerusalem to the earlier school at Salamanca. "There is in biblical studies a school of Jerusalem just as there was in the sixteenth century, in theology, a school of Salamanca;...the Dominican Father Lagrange formed students who became masters as did the Dominican Father Francisco de Vitoria, almost four centuries ago." Moreover, the influence of Father Lagrange was not confined to a circle of biblical scholars. His work served as an epistemological model to a wider community. Father Chenu drew on it for his studies in theology. Father Lebret used it in his study of economics. Both men expressed their gratitude to Father Lagrange for his inspiration.

The reputation of the School of Jerusalem as an academic institution was largely a result of Father Lagrange's publications. The school was sanctioned by official recognition when it became the French Archaeological School of Jerusalem in 1920, under the patronage of the Academy of Inscriptions and Literature. It was honored at the time of its one-hundredth anniversary by the Academy of Inscriptions, which devoted a splendid opening session to the scientific work of Father Lagrange and his disciples at the start of the academic year on November 23, 1990.

Acceptance by the Catholic Church developed more slowly. Resistance to scholarly exegesis was as unrelenting as it was prolonged. From the theological viewpoint, exegesis appeared to destroy the traditional interpretation of the Bible and to be too opposed to a routine that had become confused with tradition. Like Moses at the border of the Promised Land, Father Lagrange died without having seen the victory of the cause for which he had fought so mightily. An indication that the storm against scholarly exegesis was clearing was Pope Pius XI's appointment of Cardinal Tisserant, a former student and friend of Father Lagrange, to the Biblical Commission. The cardinal's letter of August 20, 1941, had resolutely stood up for critical exegesis. The encyclical *Divino afflante Spiritu* of September 1943 lifted the interdictions that until then had shackled biblical exegesis in the Catholic Church. According to the only historian who had access to the papers of the Biblical Commission, the secretary, Father Jacques Vosté, who was also a former student of Father Lagrange, composed the encyclical. Of this act, Father Gerard Saliège, archbishop of Toulouse, wrote on October 1944. "The Holy Father's letter is written to silence these ignorant integrists. In the heavenly mansions, the Very Reverend Father Lagrange and many others with him are singing: 'Amen. Amen. Alleluia. Alleluia!' "

Undoubtedly, Archbishop Saliège had cried victory too soon. Despite the letter of the Biblical Commission to Cardinal Suhard in January 1948, progress did not go forward in a continuous manner but through numerous rearguard actions. Only the constitution *Dei Verbum* of the Second Vatican Council, on November 18, 1965, would definitely turn the page, legitimizing a century of scientific results. In the future, research could be carried out following new ways, endorsed by the most recent document of the Biblical Commission, *The Interpretation of the Bible in the Church* (April 15, 1993). Although many new methods of interpretation came to light, none were better than the historical criticism of sacred scripture, which was fundamental. As Paul Ricoeur recently observed, "One of the greatest successes of Europe is to have a successful cohabitation of Christianity and critical thought. This combination of the revealed Word and critical reflection exists nowhere else, neither in Islam nor in the Far East" (*La croix*, March 14 to 15, 1993).

The scholarly reading of the Bible appears too often as dried, if not bitter, fruit. In reaction to this unappealing fare, a wild, careless reading of the Bible, whether of fundamentalist or of pietistic bent, far removed from the traditional *lectio divina* in the church, often results. When the Biblical Commission invites the exegete "not to limit himself either to a spiritual commentary devoid of all historical-critical basis nor to an historical-critical commentary devoid of doctrinal and spiritual content," it is only going back to the rule that guided Father Lagrange. He knew that his work would pass, but he hoped that his inspiration would live on. This was his gift: an inspiration resolutely theological that, by uniting dogma and critical thought, treats the Bible not just as a document of religious history, but as the Word of God, historically revealed to men and women.

In his lifetime, Father Lagrange felt the weight of suspicion and blame but did not lose courage. In our day, the great master of exegesis has been presented by Pope Paul VI as "a man in whom critical sagacity, faith, and attachment to the Church shine in an exceptional way" (March 14, 1974). At the time of the biblical crisis, at the beginning of the twentieth century, Father Lagrange had found the right position. At least, that is the assessment of Pope John Paul II: "Certain people, in their concern to defend the faith, thought it necessary to reject seriously established conclusions. That was a hasty and unhappy decision. The work of a pioneer like Father Lagrange was to know how to make the necessary discriminations on the basis of sound criteria" (October 31, 1992). Whenever faith and culture conflict, the synthesis of the scholar and the believer represented by Father Lagrange remains a luminous example and guide given to the church.

APPENDIX I

CONFIDENTIAL REPORT ADDRESSED TO HIS HOLINESS POPE PIUS XI BY FATHER LOUIS THEISSLING, MASTER GENERAL OF THE DOMINICANS, AFTER HIS CANONICAL VISITATION OF THE MONASTERY OF SAINT STEPHEN AT JERUSALEM

(AGOP XI, 65200)

Holy Father,

As I had the honor of saying in my previous request for an audience, I personally direct the following reflections to our venerable and beloved protector. If I am not mistaken, these reflections are of a nature to bear not only on the common good of the church but also on that religious personage of such high worth and eminent virtue who directs the Biblical School of Jerusalem.

You are not unaware, Holy Father, of the distressing suspicion under which Father Lagrange and his work have been placed on the part of several people. It seemed right to me to place before you an account of the facts that I am sure are capable of showing how much these suspicions and this disfavor are unfounded.

I note, first of all, two facts of great importance:

The first is that Father Lagrange has never published anything that has not been examined according to the laws of the church and those of his order, and that none of his writing has been put on the Index.

The second is that Father Lagrange, seeing himself the object of distressing suspicions and fearing to become an obstacle to the good of the church, which he had sought above all, often begged his superiors to relieve him of biblical studies and to apply him instead to the sacred ministry. But his superiors, always in conformity with the will of your eminent predecessors Pope Pius X and Pope Benedict XV, pushed this request aside.

It is unnecessary to recall the principles of Father Lagrange's exegetical method. They are known and completely explained in the *Revue biblique* of 1898. That same year and according to his method, a first attempt on Genesis appeared. On this subject, Bishop Esser, censor of the *Revue biblique* and theologian known for his leanings, which are anything but liberal, wrote to him: "I have seen nothing in this manuscript that can be criticized on theological grounds. But one must not forget that Catholics have neglected biblical studies for a long time. Theologians themselves, it must be acknowledged, are often little versed in the comparative history of religions. That being the case, it is to be feared that one might accuse of recklessness those who would abandon certain positions that are still in favor. Criticism, however sound and wise it may be, will not be recognized as right overnight."

Two years later, on June 17, 1900, the same eminent prelate wrote again. "One cannot deny that there is an awakening of this [exegetical] science going on. But many people do not yet see clearly and still rub their eyes....I am sure you are the man called upon to make known little by little the needs and tasks of exegesis. You have two qualities....First of all, you avoid any word that could offend, no matter whom, and even in your controversies, you are perfectly courteous;...Secondly, your style has nothing of rationalist and Protestant coldness, but betrays everywhere your heart full of faith and of your attachment to the church and to her teaching."

However, Father Lagrange's method had, since its publication, aroused rather violent opposition among these "theologians little versed in the comparative history of religions." A denunciation was even lodged at the Holy Office by Bishop Piavi, patriarch of Jerusalem. What became of it? It remained secret, naturally. But it is significant that no echo of it reached Father Lagrange.

Furthermore, in 1902, Pope Leo XIII wished to establish, in the matter of biblical criticism, the principle of competence, and he created a Biblical Commission of which Father Lagrange was named consultant. We thought that this was the definitive victory, and his Eminence, Cardinal Frühwirth, then master general, warmly congratulated the director of the Biblical School. It was, indeed, a victory, so complete that Pope Leo XIII had Father Lagrange come to Rome and had Cardinal Rampolla explain to him his plan to found a biblical institute in the Eternal City where he himself would have a distinguished place. By the same wish of the Holy Father, the *Revue biblique* would be transferred to Rome, where it would continue to enjoy all the liberty compatible with respect to Catholic principles.

Having asked for time to reflect, Father Lagrange begged, a little later on, that they would allow him to remain in obscurity at Jerusalem. But Pope Leo XIII did not consent to that, and Cardinal Rampolla wrote to him on June 22, 1903: "In this whole question, the Holy See has no other intention except to give you and your order a proof of its benevolence and of its esteem. The Institute of Higher Biblical Studies is sure that Your Fatherhood will be fully satisfied, as soon as he has been informed of the measures taken by the Holy Father in this regard....All that remains for me to do is to encourage you to continue your works for the good, and to assure Your Fatherhood of especial benevolence."

It was at the beginning of this same year, 1903, that *The Historical Method* appeared, examined by Father Frühwirth himself, and a copy of it was offered to the cardinals of the commission, without anyone making a comment about it.

Undoubtedly, Father Lagrange had...the support of the Holy See. Now, I have his formal assurance that, since that time, he has not made a step forward beyond the positions that manifestly had the approval of Pope Leo XIII.

But this same year, 1903, saw the death of the great pontiff. Almost immediately, there was a hue and cry against the *Revue biblique* and its editor. They attacked *The Historical Method* particularly. What did the Holy See think about it? They did not have to wait long to find out.

In 1906, Father Lagrange submitted his commentary on Genesis to the censors. Duly authorized, this work was sent to the printers, and they were working on chapter VI when the Sovereign Pontiff gave the order to the general, through the intermediary Cardinal Merry del Val, "that the work must not be printed, not as a volume, nor in a review, nor by way of proofs, nor in any form whatever" (Letter dated May 29, 1907). Some samples of what had already been printed were sent to the cardinals of the commission; then everything was immediately destroyed at the printers.

The Holy See in this way took a stand without, however, demanding any retraction. Understanding this situation, Father Lagrange wrote: "It seemed to me that in conscience I must only adhere to the official declarations without hesitation, which I did, and [I] witness to a complete obedience as to the general directives, which I also did in abandoning [my work on] the Old Testament and in conforming to the decisions of the Biblical Commission as to the New Testament."

Since then, Father Lagrange has published commentaries on St. Mark, on St. Paul to the Romans, on St. Paul to the Galatians, and on St. Luke, in which, up until now, not even his most sworn adversaries have found anything to reproach. These are the works I have the honor of offering to Your Holiness.

During this time the Biblical Institute which, in Pope Leo XIII's plan, should be widely opened to scholars, became a work of the Society of Jesus. Its director, the Reverend Leopold Fonck, wished soon thereafter to establish a biblical institute in the Holy Land. But St. Stephen was already there. A campaign was begun and relentlessly pursued, even in Jerusalem, to discredit the St. Stephen school and to get the public to admit the usefulness of establishing alongside of it an institute that would correspond, better than that of the Dominicans, to the spirit of the church. Following a discussion where I brought certain of these facts to the attention of your predecessor Pope Benedict XV, of blessed memory, the Holy Father said to me verbatim: "In my lifetime the Jesuit Fathers will not establish themselves in Jerusalem...unless they have a document written by my predecessors because, in that case, I would have my hands tied...but nevertheless, we will still see...."

To conclude, Holy Father, I permit myself simply to say to Your Holiness that after having closely examined the sentiments as well as the intellectual tendencies of Father Lagrange and of his collaborators, I remain convinced there is great profit for the good of the church if this Biblical School be maintained and encouraged. It cannot be bad for the church that schools of different tendencies deal, with the [aid of the] church and with perfect submission to her teaching office, with problems many of which do not touch questions of faith. Of course, some object, [saying] that we should not shock Catholic opinion...but as Father Lagrange himself writes, "You would have to be blind not to see that those occupied with sacred scripture, in the great majority, are in agreement with the *Revue biblique.* That is true even with the Society of Jesus, at least in England, France, and Belgium, without speaking of its most learned body, the Bollandists."

The École biblique counts at present eight Dominican professors and seventeen students from various orders and from various dioceses. A genuine good is done there, in a spirit of full submission to the holy church. It is thus with all my heart that I beg of Your Holiness a special blessing for the professors, the students, the works of the Biblical School of St. Stephen, and particularly for its eminent and holy director, Father Lagrange, of whom you will surely find, in the enclosed letter, Very Holy Father, the expression of a perfect and filial submission of mind and of heart.

Rome, June 23, 1922
Father Louis Theissling, OP
Master General

APPENDIX II

THE TRANFER OF THE ASHES OF FATHER LAGRANGE TO JERUSALEM

Father Lagrange died at nine o'clock Thursday morning, March 10, 1938. The funeral was celebrated Saturday the twelfth under the presidency of Monsignor Siméone, bishop of Fréjus-Toulon, assisted by Monsignor Arène, vicar general, and by Canon Martin, superior of the major seminary. Present were Monsignor Bruno de Solages, rector of the Catholic Institute of Toulouse; Andre Robert, PSS, of the Catholic Institute of Paris; Père François Marie Braun, OP, of the University of Fribourg; Prof. Jean Guitton of the University of Montpellier, accompanied by a student; Father Raymond Créchet, OP, provincial of the teaching Dominicans, former prior of St. Stephen of Jerusalem (1912 to 1914); several Dominican priors; and "a number of dignitaries and members of the clergy and of religious orders" (E. Lauzière, "The Last Moments of Father Lagrange," in *L'année dominicaine*, volume 74, number 5, May 5, 1938, pp. 140–41). A letter by Jean Guitton to Cardinal Tisserant, written the same evening, relates with emotion the last moments of Father Lagrange and his burial. The account published in *L'année dominicaine* adds that "Cardinal Liénart, the French consul at Jerusalem, a number of bishops, and several Dominican houses, as well as ecclesiastical and lay personalities had joined us in our prayers for the deceased." The letters and telegrams of condolence received on this occasion (those sent to Rome as well as those sent to St. Maximin), having been given to Père L. H. Vincent, suffered the lot common to the papers of the servant of God: They were burnt.

At Jerusalem, Thursday, March 17, a funeral service was celebrated for the repose of the soul of Father Lagrange under the presidency of the Latin patriarch and in the presence of the French consul general (reported in *L'année dominicaine*, May 1938, pp. 148–49).

The remains of Father Lagrange had been buried in the open ground in the convent cemetery located in the enclosure of the priory, in a place of honor at the center facing a little chapel, whereas the other deceased brothers were buried on either side perpendicular to the cemetery wall. Like the tombs of the other brothers, that of Father Lagrange was covered with a mound of soil; at the head was put a simple cross of black wood on which was attached an inscription engraved on a metal plaque. The text of the inscription had been requested by Father L. H. Vincent and by Father Thomas Lacrampe, prior of St. Maximin. The inscription is clearly legible on a 1942 photograph showing Friar Stève in prayer before the tomb: *"Pater Maria Josephus Lagrange, O.P./ Natus die 7a Martii MDCCCLV / Vita functus / Die 10a Martii MDCCCCXXXVIII / Scholae Biblicae Hierosolymitanae / Conditor / Sacrarum Litterarum / Indefesus interpres / Hic / in Pace Christi quiescit."* ("Father Mary Joseph Lagrange, O.P./ born March 7, 1855 / died / March 10, 1938 / founder / of the Biblical School of Jerusalem / tireless Interpreter / of the Sacred Letters / Here / he rests in the Peace of Christ.")

Of the very abundant obituary literature, it suffices to mention here the encyclical letter of Father Martin Stanislas Gillet, master of the order, dated from New York, March 28, 1938 (published in *Analecta Sacri Ordinis Praedicatorum*, XXIII, March–April 1938, pp. 414–20, original in French; Spanish translation published in *Ciencia tomista*, 29, 1938, pp. 155–60). Father Stephan Vayssière, provincial prior of the Toulouse Province, afterwards addressed his thanks to the master of the order, on May 7, 1938.

"God had given him to our province; he had kept the love of it in his heart and he wanted to come here to die and to find his final rest in this Priory of St. Maximin, cradle of his novitiate, so that our young religious, who are housed there, find in his remembrance and the presence of his remains the grace of Dominican fervor, which without fail animated his deserving and glorious life" (*AGOP*, XIII, 36104).

The transfer of the ashes of Father Lagrange to St. Stephen at Jerusalem was officially requested of Father Debroise, prior provincial of Toulouse, October 30, 1965, by Father Aniceto Fernandez, master of the order. On February 4, 1966, a provincial council to which were added the superiors of the province, meeting at Nice under the presidency of the master of the order, unanimously accepted the requested transfer (ADT, correspondence with the general curia). The agreement, having been transmitted to the prior of St. Stephen at Jerusalem by Father Pierre Benoît was the first step in the realization of this transfer, but it was still necessary to act prudently. When the Jordanian authorities on which the Biblical School (located in Jordanian territory) at that time depended had agreed to the transfer on condition that it be done very discreetly, Father de Rudder, missions procurator in Paris, was charged with working out the details with the Minister of Foreign Affairs of Paris.

In the spring of 1967, Father de Rudder had the remains of Father Lagrange exhumed and placed in a small casket made for that purpose. In the presence of his family and the Dominicans, a brief religious ceremony took place in the Basilica of St. Maximin on April 10, 1967. Then Father Benoît, delegated by the Biblical School to escort the body to Jerusalem, and Father de Rudder transported the casket in a car as far as the military aviation field of Istres. The Ministry of Foreign Affairs had granted the authorization to transport the casket "by the diplomatic pouch." Quite regularly a military plane carried mail to different embassies and legations of the Middle East. Tuesday, April 11, the casket was put on board at Istres and, after various stops, arrived at Amman

(Jordan), where a car from the Biblical School took it discreetly in charge and brought it to Jerusalem. The remains of Father Lagrange were definitively buried in the choir of St. Stephen basilica, November 13, 1967. (Please see the notes of Father de Rudder to Father de Couesnongle, master of the order, dated from the seventh to the twentieth of October 1976: *AGOP* XI, 66601.)

In remembrance of the ceremony of November 13, 1967, at St. Stephen of Jerusalem, the Biblical School keeps a photographic record: The School also keeps a typed copy of the homily given by Father Benoît. (See the following appendix.)

APPENDIX III

ALLOCUTION GIVEN BY PIERRE BENOÎT, OP, ON THE OCCASION OF THE BURIAL OF FATHER LAGRANGE IN THE BASILICA OF ST. STEPHEN AT JERUSALEM

NOVEMBER 12, 1967

Monsieur Le Consul General[1]
Monsieur Le Consul[2]
My Brothers,

The basilica consecrated to the first Christian martyr is full of the memory of Père Lagrange. He closely followed the excavation of the ancient church of the fifth century and the building of the new church. He devoted the first of his numerous books to the story of St. Stephen and of his shrine. For almost fifty years, he prayed here, coming between two works to rest his soul, to warm his heart, to enlighten his spirit near the master who resides here. The oldest among us remember having seen him, at the end of each morning, recollect himself here in great silence, at the foot of the tabernacle and of Mary.

His great age and his illnesses obliged him to return to France and he died there, in the Priory of St. Maximin, where he had taken

---

1. Baron Christian d'Halloy, French consul general in Jerusalem
2. Michel André, French consul in Jerusalem

the habit of the Preachers and lived the first years of his religious life. For almost thirty years, he slept in the little cemetery in the shadow of the old basilica restored to the order by Father Lacordaire. However, almost all of his old companions in the struggle reposed at St. Stephen: Father Matthew Lecomte, founder of the monastery, and the other fathers of the first team, then the disciples of Father Lagrange, Fathers Vincent, Savignac, Abel, all the way to the humble lay brothers who helped to found this house. The sons of the second generation regretted that Father Lagrange did not also repose among them, close by all those dear older men of whom he had been the leader and the inspirer.

The circumstances having become favorable, they were finally able to realize their desire. With the willing and generous assistance of the French government, the exhumation and the transfer were accomplished last April. The burial in this basilica was supposed to be carried out June 5. The course of events [the Six-Day War between Israel and the Arabs] thwarted this plan, and we postponed the ceremony until the beginning of the new school year. That is what gathers us together this morning in an intimate and familial group of friends, of disciples, of disciples of the disciples in the presence of the representative of France. The French government greatly aided Father Lagrange in his work just as France always found in him a loving and devoted son.

His burial in the center of the choir of our basilica is meant to be, first of all, a gesture of filial piety, homage to the memory of the venerated founder of the Biblical School, a means of keeping his memory alive.

No doubt these poor bones are not very important, these bones which have been found intertwined with the roots of a cedar tree. Undoubtedly, Father Lagrange is something altogether different and present in a completely different manner. He is present in God, in union with Christ—we are confident of that; present in our hearts who love and admire him; present by his writings and by his work in so many minds that he has helped to see the issues clearly and to keep the faith.

But we are creatures of the senses and our thoughts need material support. The presence of these mortal remains under a slab, whose inscription evokes who he was and what he did, will unceasingly recall his living memory to his younger brothers who will pray in this church, to the students who will attend his school, to the visitors and to the pilgrims of St. Stephen who will want to add to the memory of the first martyr that of another witness to the faith.

For the living memory of Father Lagrange ought to be rich in lessons for his sons, and the concern to better imitate his examples is another reason for this burial that is going to concretize his presence among us.

I am not going to attempt a proper panegyric of his virtues. That is neither possible nor necessary. In fact, do we not have at present in our hands those memoirs of his which were just published and which disclose to us in a very moving way the secret recesses of his soul and of his life?

Allow me simply to evoke rapidly three traits that seem to me to be particularly salient and that I would like to see etched in our memories as the precious result of this ceremony.

First of all, consider his apostolic zeal. One is struck in contemplating his life and in rereading his memoirs by the care that inspires all his moves, to serve God in working for the salvation of his brothers. It is for this that he sought the priesthood and put on the livery of St. Dominic. There is nothing in him of the dilettante nor of the detached scholar who only wishes to satisfy his thirst for knowledge. If he studies, if he teaches, it is solely in the service of the truth, according to the motto of his order, and of this truth as it is revealed to us by God himself in his words of sacred scripture, which was the passion of his entire life. If he so loved this Word and wrote so much about it, it was above all and always to help men hear it and to find God.

He searched for this truth and communicated it with a faith as strong and deep as it was intelligent and enlightened. This is the second trait I want to recall. Everyone knows what astute and critical intelligence was his. It sufficed to meet him, and still now it suffices to read him, to recognize it immediately. But it must not be forgotten that this exacting reason, hungry for scientific guarantees, for rigor in knowledge, was always allied in him with an ardent, strong, simple faith that guided all his thought processes. If he succeeded better than others in renewing Catholic exegesis by using the historical method without ruining doctrinal truths but, on the contrary, by fortifying them in all sorts of ways, it was because he never admitted the fatal divorce of reason from faith. His efforts of critical research were always guided and assured by this abandonment to the Word and to the Spirit, which alone procures true light.

He could only do it because he was humble and obedient. This is the third trait I want to underline. I do not think only of that humility among his brothers, even among those who were truly inferior, which made his company so pleasant, nor only of that obedience toward his superiors which kept him as a docile child in their hands. I think of that humility of spirit and of that inner obedience which allowed him to submit himself sincerely and completely to the magisterium of the church and to hear without complaint so many false suspicions of which his good faith had been the object. Everyone knows the hard battles he had to fight. If he triumphed over poorly founded opposition and if he always followed the directives of the church, certainly without abdicating anything of the truth as he saw it, but in searching only to see it better, it was that he was more than intelligent and scholarly: He was meek and humble of heart.

Such are the great lessons that he leaves us. Such are the examples that we will have at heart to follow. Gathered in prayer around his tomb, sure that he is still among us and prays with us, we will pray with him, so that God grants us, his modest disciples, and all our colleagues in the field of sacred scripture, and all the sons and daughters of the church, to overcome, as he did, the crises of faith that still rage in our day, and to work as he did, honestly, clearly, courageously, humbly, in the service of the Word.

He said of himself on his death memento: "Son of the church that he desired to serve." Dear Father Lagrange, you have served your mother, the church, well, and your mother the church has officially recognized it. By your prayers obtain for us the grace to serve her in our turn, for the glory of God the Father, in the light of the Son, and in the power of the Spirit.

Amen.

APPENDIX IV

THE FAMILY BACKGROUND OF FATHER LAGRANGE

The Lagranges were of peasant origin. The land in which they were rooted and that they cultivated is located in Charolais, around St.-Romain-sous-Gourdon (in Saône-et-Loire, District of Chalon-sur-Saône, Canton of Mont-St.-Vincent). Father Lagrange's grandfather, Louis (1786–1866), was first a landowner in the hamlet of the Moulins, as was his great-grandfather, Benoît (born in 1755), and then in the hamlet of Prat in the same commune of St.-Romain, where he was mayor in the year 1820. "My grandfather was a peasant who had by persistent work succeeded in creating a rather beautiful estate. He had enough influence as town mayor to obtain the reestablishment of the parish, under the Restoration. He had remained very attached to that Regime." His grandmother, Antoinette-Philippe Cléau (1789–1873), came from the same rural region and belonged to the same social milieu. By their great-grandmother, Jeanne Aumonier, the Lagranges were linked, at least this was the family tradition, to St. Margaret Mary Alacoque: Her brother, Chrysostome, had married Angélique Aumônier in 1666. Peasant but not, therefore, boorish. "The sentiments of my Lagrange grandparents had an innate high character and nobility that characterized, in old France, the Christian peasants, to the point of striking a young English observer with admiration."

Six children were born of their marriage: Jeanne in 1812, married in 1840 to Jean Langeron, whose son Joseph (1840–1921) would be a priest in the Diocese of Autun; Claude-Pierre in 1814, who would become notary at Bourg-en-Bresse;

Marie Françoise in 1816, religious of St. Charles at Lyons, god-mother of Father Lagrange; Philibert in 1818, deceased five months later; Claude-Marie in 1819, who would take over the family property at Prat; Louis-Jean in 1825, who would become a priest in 1851 and would be pastor of St.-Romain-sous-Gourdon in 1858. He would be one of the first subscribers to the *Revue biblique*. He died in 1896.

Claude-Pierre, the oldest boy, was one of the country boys the priests directed toward the seminary of Autun to assure after-wards, they hoped, their replacement in the parishes: "intelli-gences still rough-hewn but vigorous, and judiciously chosen by the pastors among those who were the most gifted and sons of sin-cerely Christian families." The description that Father Lagrange gave of his own friends at the seminary of Autun is equally valid for his father's generation. But Claude-Pierre, once gone from the minor to the major seminary, perceived that he was not called to become a priest as he had thought, and so turned toward the post of notary clerk. The path of social ascent, passing through the seminary of Autun, was going to make the country boy from Burgundy a Bressan notary. A generation later, Father Lagrange observed at Autun the same system of promotion: "Those who did not enter the major seminary and did not return to the plow because they felt drawn by a higher ambition, turned toward Lyons, most frequently to study medicine. My father followed the career of notary." Ambition alone did not suffice to gain the posi-tion of first clerk at Lyons. It was necessary to possess the means: One could not do it unless he had means, such as did the Lagranges of St.-Romain. It was at Lyons also that Claude-Pierre met Élisabeth Falsan, whom he would marry in 1850.

The Falsans belonged to the business world: that of bour-geois notables, manufacturers, and merchants; for generations they were part of the Lyons elite. Further back, they descended from a Montpellier family of cloth merchants, of which the first known, Gilles Falsan (1603–1678), buried in the family tomb at the Church of the Franciscan Observance, had married

Antoinette Brous (1609–1679), buried in the cemetery of the Gentlemen of the Reformed Religion. (What malevolent conclusions the adversaries of Father Lagrange would have drawn from his Huguenot descent if they had only known!) Their grandson Jean (1685–1768), born at Montpellier, came to Lyons to be married and to settle there in the beginning of the eighteenth century.

In 1822, the grandfather, Pierre-Honoré Falsan (1795–1867), had married Josephine Chavanes of Bagnois (1805–1831), of a family "always very honorably known at Lyons," by whom he had two daughters: Amélie-Claudine (1823–1887) married to Dr. Ariste Potton, and Élisabeth (1827–1902) married to Claude-Pierre Lagrange. From a second marriage in 1832 to Thérèse Niepce (1810–1902), daughter of a colonel, he had a son Albert (1833–1902), the geologist, and godfather of Father Lagrange. Later, the children of Aunt Amélie Potton and those of Uncle Albert Falsan would be on cordial familiar terms with the children of Claude-Pierre Lagrange.

BIBLIOGRAPHY

Additional Publications on Père Lagrange by Bernard Montagnes, OP

"La condition de l'exégèse catholique au temps du modernisme: Le Père Lagrange." *Revue thomiste* 87 (1987): 533–46.

"Un témoignage inédit du Père Lagrange sur le Père Cormier." *DocOP* 23 (1988): 55–58 [previously in *Concorde* no. 129 (December 1987): 13–16.]

"Il 50° del fondatore della scuola biblica de Gerusalemme, Marie-Joseph Lagrange, servitore della Parola de Dio." *L'osservatore romano* (Friday, March 11, 1988). [In French in *L'edition hebdomadaire en langue française* (April 5, 1988): 4.]

"Le Père Marie-Joseph Lagrange, serviteur de la Parole de Dieu." *Sources* (Fribourg) 14 (1988): 187–90.

"Le rétablissement de l'Ordre des Prêcheurs à Jérusalem: du couvent Saint-Étienne a l'École biblique." *AFP* 58 (1988): 361–422.

"Deux lettres du Père Hugues Vincent au sujet du Père Lagrange." *Sources* (Fribourg) 14 (1989): 137–41.

"Au temps du modernisme: deux lettres de Robert Beudant au Père Lagrange." *DocOP* 24 (1989): 56–60.

"Un fidèle dévot à Marie: Le Père Marie-Joseph Lagrange." *Revue du rosaire* (July 1989): 189–202.

"Premiers combats du Père Lagrange: Le Congrès de Fribourg 1897." *AFP* 59 (1989): 287–369.

Exégèse et obéissance. Correspondance Cormier-Lagrange 1904–1916. Introduced, edited, and commented on by Bernard Montagnes, OP, preface by Jean Guitton, of l'Académie française, Paris, Gabalda, 1989. Work honored by l'Académie française (Prix Monthyon 1990).

"La postérité de Lacordaire [le P. Lagrange]." *Mélanges de l'École française de Rome, Italie, Méditerranée* 101 (1989): 451–68 [published in 1990].

"Le Père Lagrange: la figure du savant et du croyant." *Préfaces, les idées et les sciences dans la bibliographie de la france* no. 16 (December 1989–January 1990): 72–74.

"Les séquelles de la crise moderniste: l'École biblique au lendmain de la grande guerre." *Revue thomiste* 90 (1990): 245–70.

"Combats pour une histoire de la bible." *L'histoire* no. 133 (May 1990): 64–67.

"Les lettres du P. Lagrange à Mgr. de Solages 1925–1937." *Bulletin de littérature ecclésiastique* 91 (1990): 83–100.

"L'École biblique de Jérusalem ou le grand dessein du Père Lagrange." *France catholique* no. 2264 (July 6, 1990): 22–23.

"À Saint-Étienne de Jérusalem. Le centenaire de l'École biblique." *Oeuvre d'Orient* no. 673 (December 1990): 527–29.

"Frère Thomas Tabin, convers à l'École biblique de Jérusalem." *DocOp* no. 25 (1990).

"Le Père Lagrange et la fondation de l'École biblique et archéologique française de Jérusalem." *Bulletin mensuel de l'Académie de Vaucluse* no. 223 (April 1991): 3–4.

"Premiers combats du Père Lagrange: les conférences de Toulouse 1902." *AFP* 61 (1991): 355–413.

"Témoignages au sujet du Père Lagrange 1912 et 1938." *DocOP* no. 27 (Nouvelle Série): 3–15.

"Le Père Lagrange ou la miséricorde de la vérité." *La vie spirituelle* no. 699 (March–April 1992): 191–200.

"L'ascendant du Père Lagrange, un maître en théologie, le Père Marie-Michel Labourdette, O. P." *Revue thomiste* 92 (1992): 52–58.

"La méthode historique: succès et revers d'un manifeste." *Naissance de la méthode critique*, Congrès du centenaire de l'École biblique et archéologique française de Jérusalem, Paris, Éd. du Cerf (1992): 67–88.

"En marge du Portrait du Père Lagrange par Jean Guitton." *Mémoire dominicaine, I, fondateurs-fondatrices.* Paris: Éd. du Cerf, (1992): 185–88.

"L'année terrible du Père Lagrange d'après les lettres à E. Tisserant." *AFP* 62 (1992): 324–83.

"Le thomisme du Père Lagrange." *Ordo sapientiae et amoris*, Image et message de Saint Thomas d'Aquin à travers les récentes études historiques, herméneutiques et doctrinales, hommage au Professeur Jean-Pierre Torrell O.P., à l'occasion de son 65e anniversaire, Fribourg, Switzerland (1993): 487–508.

"L'ultime chagrin du Père M. J. Lagrange." *Revue des sciences philosophiques et theologiques* 78 (1994): 3–29.

"Marie Joseph Lagrange: la figure du savant et du croyant." *Nouvelle revue theologique* 116 (1994): 715–26.

"La correspondance du Père Lagrange avec l'Abbé Bardy." *Mélanges de science religieuse* 52 (1995): 65–86.

"L'Abbé Lusseau contre la *Revue thomiste.*" [Un disciple de Père Bea contre un disciple de Père Lagrange]. In *Saint Thomas au XXe siècle*, Actes du colloque du centenaire de la *Revue thomiste* (March 25–28, 1993). Toulouse: sous la direction du Père Serge-Thomas Bonino O.P.; Paris: Éd. Saint-Paul (1994 [1995]): 122–33.

"Ernest Renan selon le Père Lagrange." *Revue thomiste* 95 (1995): 273–83.

Le Père Lagrange (1855–1938), l'exégèse catholique dans la crise moderniste. Paris: Éd. du Cerf, 1995.

"La question biblique au temps de Pie XI." In *Achille Ratti Pape Pie XI*, Actes du colloque organisé par l'École française de Rome (Rome, March 15–18, 1989), Rome, École française, 1996: 255–76.

"Lagrange." *Dictionnaire du monde religieux dans la France contemporaine, 9, les sciences religieuses.* Paris: Beauchesne, (1996): 355–68.

"L'amitié Batiffol-Lagrange." *Bulletin de litterature ecclésiastique* 98 (1997): 3–20.

"Les 'Logia' du Père Lagrange." *Mémoire dominicaine*, no. 10 (Spring 1997): 165–81.

"Les années d'initiation dominicaine du Père Lagrange ou l'apprentissage de l'humilité (1879–1884)." *Revue thomiste* 97 (1997): 355–68.

"Lagrange." *Dictionnaire de biographie française*, vol. XIX, fascicule CX, col.: 282–84.

"La crise de la *Revue biblique* en 1898–1899." *Archivum Fratrum Praedicatorum* 67 (1997): 345–79.